Endorsements

Strikingly relatable and beautifully sincere, this story doesn't rush the healing process—it respects it. A must-read for anyone navigating the quiet battle of rebuilding self-worth.

— Tiffany Latoya Forbes

A powerful and raw exploration of trauma, healing, and spiritual transformation. Pastor Kim's story is both deeply personal and universally relatable—a testament to the resilience of the human spirit and the restorative work of the Holy Spirit.

— Natalie Blake

The Little Girl Within

Kimberely R. Allen

Foreword by Dr. Kemberly E. McKenzie
Cover Design by Wendi Hayman
Edited by Nicole M. Queen

Allen Ministries Publishing Company

Allen Ministries Publishing Company
Fort Washington, MD

ISBN: 979-8-218-70752-1 (print)
LCCN: 2025911997

This book is established to provide information and inspiration to all readers. It is
designed with the understanding that the author is not engaged to render any
psychological, legal, or any other kind of professional advice. The content is the sole
expression of the author. The author is not liable for any physical, psychological,
emotional, financial, or commercial damages, including, but not limited to special,
incidental, consequential, or other damages. All readers are responsible for their own
choices, actions, and results.

To the woman who's still standing after the storm,
still healing after the heartbreak,
and still hoping even when it hurts—
this is for you.

Author's Note

Writing this novel has been both deeply therapeutic and profoundly challenging. To lay bare the most vulnerable and painful aspects of my life—to confront the ghosts of my past—demanded a level of courage I never knew I possessed. Yet, in sharing my story, I discovered a strength I never imagined possible.

This is more than a chronicle of trauma; it is a testament to the resilience of the human spirit. It is a story of healing, forgiveness, and self-discovery, even when the odds seem insurmountable. Through these pages, you will witness raw emotion, heartbreak, and struggle—but also triumph, hope, and the unwavering determination to rise above.

My greatest hope is that these words resonate with you, offering solace, encouragement, and a sense of community. If you have ever felt alone in your hurt, may this book remind you that healing is possible—even when it seems impossible.

This is more than a novel. It is a beacon of hope. A reminder that your story is not over.

You may not be who they expected, but you are exactly who God intended.

— Kimberely R. Allen

Contents

Foreword

Dr. Kemberly E. McKenzie

In these pages, you will not find a fairytale version of healing. Instead, you will walk alongside a woman named Kyra, a mirror for so many of us—whose journey is stitched together with pain, questions, resilience, and ultimately, redemption. You will hear the whispers of shame, the echoes of rejection, and the silence of wounds long buried. But more importantly, you will witness what it looks like to rise one breath, one step, one brave truth at a time.

What makes this story so powerful isn't just its honesty, it is the courage it took to write it. Kimberely R. Allen has not simply invited us into a narrative; she has opened a door to her most vulnerable spaces so that we might find our own. With unwavering authenticity, she offers a lifeline to every woman who has ever felt invisible, unheard, or unworthy.

In one of the most stirring moments of the book, Kyra writes:

> *"I almost let the weight of expectations, disappointments, and unhealed wounds bury you beneath a version of yourself*

that was never meant to exist... But survival is not the same as freedom. And now, I choose freedom."

That is what this book is: a declaration of freedom. A refusal to remain buried under someone else's version of who we are allowed to be. A letter not just from Kyra—but to every woman who has been called to more. This book meets the reader in her silence and walks her into freedom.

This book is for the woman who still smiles, while bleeding. The one who shows up, even when no one knows how heavy the burden is. The one who is tired of pretending she is okay. It is for the quiet warriors. Weary believers. The hopeful healers. The ones who are still standing, even when they don't know how.

As someone who has lived, written, and coached through seasons of personal transformation, I know what it takes to share your truth when it costs you everything. Kimberely R. Allen does just that, and she does it with fierce grace.

As you turn each page, you'll be reminded that healing is not a destination but a decision, a daily, grace-filled, imperfect choice to keep going. You will see that your pain does not disqualify you from the purpose, it prepares you for it. Also, you will discover that sometimes the most sacred stories are not shouted, they are whispered in the dark, with tears and trembling hands, by women who choose to rise anyway.

If you have ever questioned your worth, if you have ever felt like your story was too messy or your wounds were too deep, this book is your permission to believe again. To breathe again. To begin again. Let the words meet you where you are.

So, take a breath. Let this story break something open in you.

And remember: To the woman reading this who has spent years waiting for someone else to set her free—hear me clearly: your freedom is not in their hands. It never was.

— Dr. Kemberly E. McKenzie

Author of
K.E.M. (Keep Everything Moving): Letting Adversity Guide You to Destiny,
Mind Your Manuscript: A Writing Guide for Emerging Authors and Amazon
Bestsellers, and Night Vision: How to See Your Way Through Any Situation

Ph.D., Educational Leadership | Personal Development Life Coach
M.A. Candidate, Clinical Mental Health Counseling
Atlanta, Georgia – June 2025

Introduction

Some stories aren't born in the spotlight—
they're written from the scars.

For every woman who has carried the invisible weight of childhood
wounds,
the ache of rejection,
or the silence of abuse—
and still found a reason to rise.

For the quiet warriors.
The ones who smile while bleeding.
Who keep showing up, even when no one sees the battle within.

You are not alone.

Writing this story wasn't easy.
It was painful.
It was honest.
But above all—
it was necessary.

These pages hold more than memories.
They hold moments—
of awakening,
of truth,
of transformation.

This isn't just my story.
It's ours.
A story marked by trauma—yes—
but also by healing.
By hope.
By the breath that returns after life has knocked the wind from your
lungs.

In these pages, you'll meet Kyra.
A woman who, for too long, carried names that didn't belong
to her—
fear, shame, unworthy.

But Kyra means noble leader.
A name that speaks of strength cloaked in grace,
of someone born to rise, even when buried beneath brokenness.
It means light, throne, and power—
a reminder that authority can be reclaimed,
and royalty can emerge from ruin.

This is the story of how she rose into that name.
How she stepped into her identity, reclaimed her voice, and dared to
lead herself out of it.

She didn't always feel strong.
She didn't always feel seen.
But every step she took became a quiet rebellion against the lies that
once defined her.

You'll also meet Rose.

The voice of shame that haunted her.
The inner critic many of us know too well.
Perhaps you've heard her whisper, too.

But hear this—
healing is possible.

Even if you don't feel ready.
Even if you're still crying in the dark.
Even if the wound still stings.

Healing doesn't demand perfection.
Only presence.

If these words find you,
then you've already refused to quit.
That alone is sacred.

So take a deep breath.
This is your invitation to exhale.
To stop running.
To face the voice.
And to find your own.

Let every chapter be a mirror.
Let every affirmation be a promise.
Let every word remind you:
You are already becoming whole.

You don't have to be loud to be healed.
You just have to be honest.

And healing will meet you there.

Welcome to your journey.

Chapter 1

I Found Healing in the Most Unexpected Places

Kyra never imagined healing would look like this.

It didn't arrive wrapped in closure.
It didn't knock politely or wait for permission.
It showed up in the quiet—
in the middle of the night,
when the house was still,
and her heart felt too full to sleep.

It came after the apology she never got.
While folding clothes.
While holding a T-shirt she hadn't worn in years—
and suddenly, unraveling in the memory it carried.

Healing didn't ask.
It entered uninvited,
ugly and inconvenient,
and made itself comfortable at the kitchen table
like it had always lived there.

She used to think healing meant the hurt had stopped.
But now—
she knew better.

Healing wasn't the absence of pain.
It was the presence of peace
in the middle of it.

It was subtle.
It was sacred.
It was slow.

It looked like finally telling the truth
when someone asked, "How are you?"
Like feeling grief—
and not rushing it.
Like remembering the wound—
without bleeding.

She had just come back from the hospital.

Nothing major, they said.
A routine procedure.
In and out.

But no one warned her
how loud the stillness would feel
once the anesthesia wore off.
No one told her the quiet could ache
deeper than the stitches.

She dropped her bag by the door.
Kicked off her shoes.
Sank into the center of the couch—
unsure what to do next.

The house felt like it had been waiting.
Not the way a loved one waits—
but the way trauma does.
Patient.
Present.
Familiar.

Sill in her oversized sweats she wore to the procedure,
she laid back on the couch,
a cushion under her arms,
her head tilted toward the ceiling—
as if it might offer answers.

Her body was sore,
but it wasn't her limbs that ached the most.

It was the buried places.
The thoughts that surfaced while she was unconscious.
The memories that floated in while her body slept.

And for once,
she didn't reach for the remote.
Didn't turn on the music.
Didn't call anyone.

She just laid there.
Awake.
Alone.
Aware.

This… was healing?
Not dancing.
Not shouting.
Not testifying.
Just— breathing.
Facing the things she'd spent years outrunning.

The anesthesia was gone,
but something else was still numbing her—
old words,
unspoken grief,
the kind of tired that sleep couldn't reach.

She closed her eyes and declared,
"God... I don't even know what to say."

And maybe that was the point.

For so long, she thought healing required the right words.
But now she was learning—
it only required honest ones.

She didn't pray aloud.
Didn't quote scripture.
She just let the tears rise.

Not all at once—
but slow.
One by one.
Testing the air
like they weren't sure they belonged.

And then came a breath.
A deep one.

Not because she was better.
But because she was still here.

And that mattered.

That—was healing.
Not perfection.
Not applause.

Just sitting in her own skin
without trying to escape it.

That's when Rose crept in.

"You're still broken.
Look at you.
Needing rest for something so small.
This isn't healing—it's weakness."

Kyra blinked.
And for a moment—
she almost believed her.

Almost.

But then came a thought.
Not loud.
Not confident.
But real.

"No... this is what healing looks like.
And you don't get to define it anymore."

She didn't say it with fire.
She said it with fatigue.

But even that was a win.

Because healing didn't look like the woman who had all the answers.
It looked like the one finally asking the right questions.

It looked like hearing criticism
without letting it cut.
Like holding the weight of generational wounds
without being crushed by them.

Like carrying bitterness in one hand—
but choosing not to wear it as armor.

It looked like showing up
with nothing left to prove.
Like having nothing else to lose—
except the lie
that she wasn't already enough.

It looked like laughter, too.
Not the kind that hides hurt.
But the kind that breaks through it.
That makes space
for joy to re-enter the room.

She reached for her journal—
not to write a sermon,
not to craft a statement—
just to name the moment.

"Today, healing looked like quiet.
Like letting the tears come without shame.
Like sitting still long enough to hear myself think.
Like *not* running."

She closed the book,
pulled the blanket over her lap,
and exhaled.

She hadn't imagined it would look like this.

But now that she was here,
she was willing to stay
long enough
to see what it might become.

Because sometimes,
the loudest evidence of healing
is simply being able to sit in the place that once undid you—
and live.

And Kyra was breathing.
Still sore.
Still uncertain.
But breathing.

And for today—
that was enough.

She was free.

Reflection:

Healing is not always a dramatic transformation or a shouted testimony. Sometimes, it's found in the stillness.

Sometimes, healing looks like:

- Choosing to sit with your emotions instead of numbing them
- Saying "I'm not okay" without shame
- Breathing deep, even when your heart is heavy
- Admitting you're not healed, but you're still here

Ask yourself:

- What does healing look like in this season of your life?
- Are you waiting for it to be loud—when it may already be whispering?
- What pain have you been afraid to sit with quietly?

Please use the space below to record your thoughts:

_____

_____

_____

_____

_____

_____

_____

_____

_____

_____

_____

_____

_____

_____

* * *

"I am walking through unfamiliar doors, and still—I am healing. Even when healing wears a different face, it is mine to embrace, slowly and fully."

Chapter 2

I Can Face the Pain I Once Tried to Hide

Kyra never asked to come into the world like this.

Her mother never made it to the delivery room.
There were no doctors standing by.
No nurse rushing to her side.
No soft blankets or warm welcomes.

She entered the world on the cold, hard floor
of an emergency room lobby.
Unplanned.
Unexpected.
And, in her young mind—unwanted.

She learned the story later,
when she was old enough to understand what rejection felt like.
Old enough to sense when love was absent.
Old enough to wonder if she was ever truly meant to be here at all.

Maybe that's why she had always felt like she was fighting
for space in a world that never made room for her.

Her childhood wasn't a collage of lullabies or laughter.
Love was something she watched on TV—
not something she had in her home.
It belonged to other children,
the ones who came to school clean and confident,
who talked about sleepovers and family vacations.
Not her.

Her father was a force of destruction.
The kind that didn't pass quietly.
He broke things—walls, dishes, trust.

And her mother,
the one who should've been her refuge,
was too cracked by her own pain
to notice the bleeding in her daughter's eyes.

Affection didn't live in their home.
It wasn't spoken.
It wasn't implied.
It didn't even know the address.

Kyra learned early that pain was a language.
That saying nothing was a response.
That survival meant swallowing screams
until they tasted like normal.

And then—there was him.
Family.
Blood.
The kind of man who entered the house without knocking,
and left pieces of her behind every time he did.

He came with a dirty fifty cents in one hand
and destruction in the other.

"Clean my room," he said.
"I'll give you a little change."

She cleaned.
He gave.
Then, he touched.
Then, he spoke.
Then he stole moments in the dark corners of the house
while no one was watching.

She was only eight.

Too young to name it abuse.
Too innocent to recognize betrayal.
She only knew attention.
And in her undeveloped mind,
she mistook destruction for love.

Until it wasn't.

Until her childhood was fractured.
Until shame crept in like a shadow.
Until her mirror no longer reflected a little girl,
but someone tainted— different.

She began to think things no child should think.
She studied the women on TV—
how they moved, how they were wanted.
Admired. Desired.

Maybe, she thought,
if I gave men what they wanted,
I'd never feel powerless again.

And then came the voice.

Rose.

A soft voice,
then a murmur,
then a constant echo.

"You're different now."
"You're damaged."
"No one will ever truly love you."

It was a lie she understood well.
One passed down like an unspoken legacy
from the people who were supposed to protect her.

So, she tried to outrun the ache.
Tried to control the pain the only way she knew how—
by giving herself away before anyone else could take her.

And she listened.

Years passed.
But the wound stayed open.

Rejection.
Shame.
Fear.

They followed her—
attaching themselves into every decision,
every relationship,
every opportunity she let slip by
because the lie had convinced her
she was never worthy to begin with.

So, she became a woman.

A paradox.
Beautiful and broken.
Admired and aching.
A woman who turned heads when she walked into the room—
tall, elegant, stunning.
But still dragging the sound of childhood behind her heels.

She poured out for others.
Gave freely.
Loved deeply.

But when the lights dimmed
and the noise of the day faded,
the soft voice still came.

Until now.

Something was shifting.

She was tired.
Tired of pretending.
Tired of surviving.
Tired of hearing Rose's voice louder than God's.

She didn't want the quiet anymore.
She wanted healing.
Real healing.

Not the kind that numbs.
The kind that roots.
That breaks chains.
That severs generational cycles and names the pain for what it is.

And she knew only One could do it.

God.

The God she prayed to—
but never trusted with her full story.
The God she sang about—
but never surrendered her secrets to.

Could He really take all of this?
The shame?
The silence?
The hidden bruises and silent screams?

Could He still use her—
even now?

She had to find out.
She was ready.

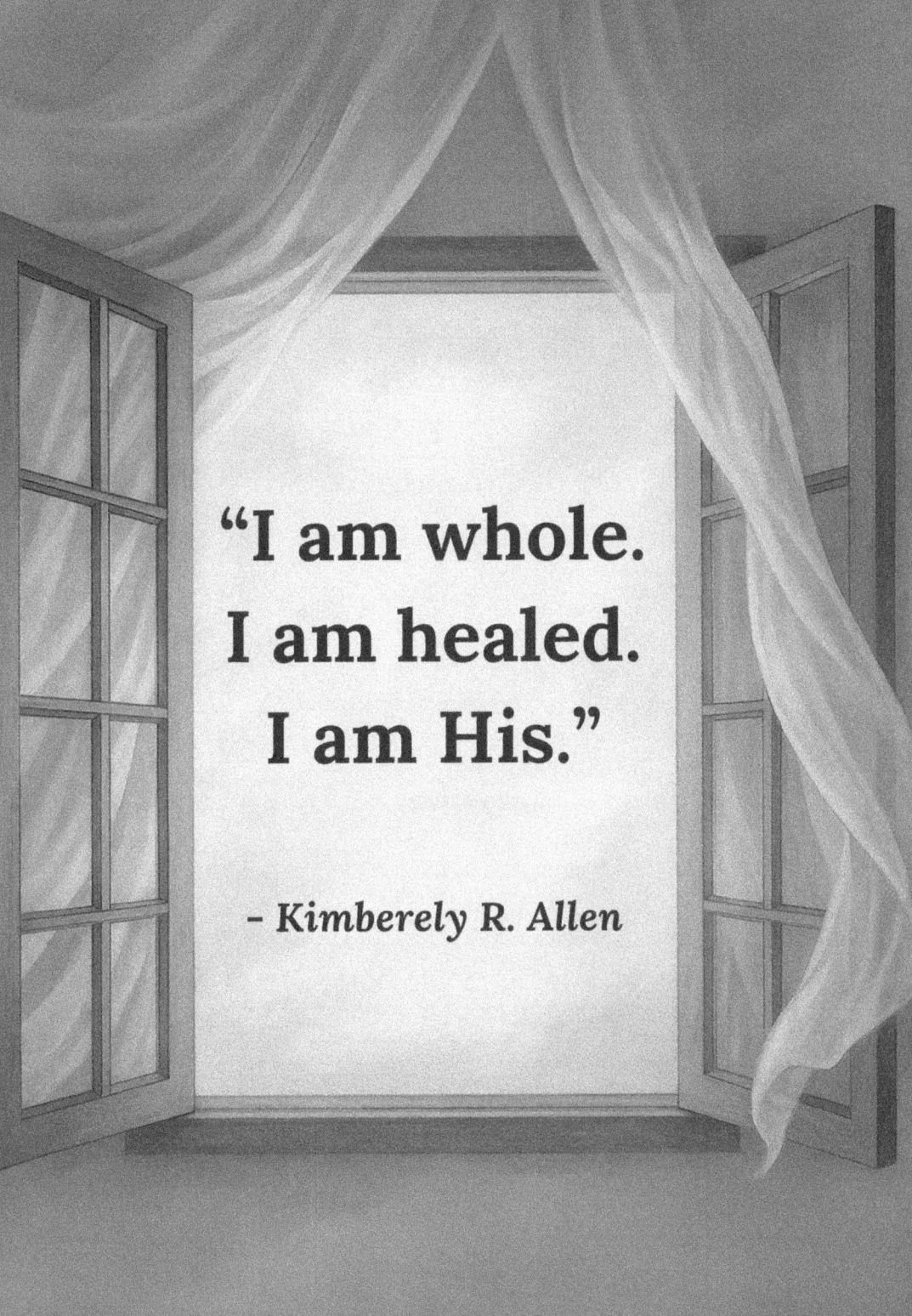

"I am whole.
I am healed.
I am His."

– Kimberely R. Allen

Reflection:

The path to healing often begins with naming the sorrow. What once kept your voice muted loses its power when you put words to it.

Bruises hide in the unnamed corners of our past—but truth shines a light.

Consider this:

- Have you given your hurt a name, or have you tried to bury it?
- What have you mistaken for love, attention, or approval that was actually harm?
- Are there voices from your past still whispering lies into your present?

You don't have to keep quiet to survive anymore.
You have permission to speak what hurt you.
To say it out loud. To call it what it was.
That's not weakness—that's warfare.

Please use the space below to record your thoughts:

_____
_____
_____
_____
_____
_____
_____
_____
_____
_____

_____
_____
_____
_____
_____
_____
_____
_____
_____
_____
_____
_____
_____
_____
_____
_____
_____
_____
_____
_____
_____
_____
_____
_____
_____
_____
_____
_____

* * *

"I am no longer afraid to speak what hurt me. Naming the pain doesn't break me
—it frees me. I am not my wound; I am my healing."

Chapter 3

I Am No Longer Owned by the Voice of My Past

Success. Visible. Shadowed.

Backstage at New York Fashion Week— again.

Twice, her designs had walked the runway.
Crafted with intention for tall women
who knew what it meant to be overlooked.
Her name printed on the program.
Her vision stitched into every thread.
Her brilliance— undeniable.

She had made it.

The clapping thundered.
Cameras flashed.
Clients smiled.

But so did Rose.

Not in the open—

but in the quiet corners of her mind.

"They just needed someone different."
"You're not as innovative as they are."
"You won't be remembered next season."
"They'll figure out you don't belong here."

Kyra had heard it all before.
In the dressing room.
While sketching patterns.
On the drive into Manhattan.
Even in the moments that were supposed to feel like victory.

And that's what no one saw—
on the outside, she was polished.
But inside, her mind was still a battlefield.

Beneath the surface, a war was raging.

She had done the unthinkable.

Became a mother before she became a woman.
Dropped out of school at seventeen.
Earned her GED in the still, quiet hours when the world was
sleeping.
Went to college—not once, but twice.
Earned her bachelor's. Then her master's.
Studied while raising a child.
Pushed through exhaustion, shame, and the slow ache of
uncertainty.

They called her strong.
Said she was an overcomer.
A force.

But even triumph couldn't drown out the voice

that met her in the muted air.

"You're still behind."
"Don't forget your mistakes."
"No one really sees the real you."
"You're not truly whole."

That was Rose.

She didn't just accuse— she advised.
She didn't scream— she suggested.
Disguised as logic.
Wrapped in caution.
Spoke through the mask of humility.

Maybe that's why Kyra let her stay so long—
Because in a life that taught her to brace for sorrow,
Rose felt like protection.

People ask—sometimes aloud, more often in the silence—
"Why did she let the voice stay so long?"

And the honest answer?

Because she didn't know she had the authority to ask it to leave.
Because when trauma is the first to speak,
truth sounds like a stranger.
Because Rose was familiar.
And familiar felt safe.
And safe felt necessary for survival.

Because culture taught her to perform—
To be excellent without ever feeling enough,
To show up without being too loud,
To succeed without revealing her scars.

So she carried success in her arms,
But bore the weight of the voice on her back.

Every mistake.
Every missed opportunity.
Every relationship she self-sabotaged—
It wasn't fear of failure.

It was Rose.

"Don't get too close."
"Don't try too hard."
"They'll leave you like the others."

And Kyra listened—not for lack of faith,
But because heartache had been her consistent teacher.

Then, something shifted.

She stopped praying just to be healed.
She started asking for a transformed mind.

A mind no longer cluttered by comparison.
No longer clouded by her past.
A mind where God's voice no longer had to compete.

And in that clarity,
She could finally answer the questions that once haunted her:

Am I enough? — Yes. I always was.
Do I belong in these rooms? — I do. And I've earned it.
If I stop pretending, will they still love me? — The right ones will.
The rest were never mine to keep.

This wasn't deliverance as she imagined—
not loud, not sudden.

It was quiet.
But it was clear.

And clarity—real, soul-deep clarity—
was the one thing Rose couldn't survive.

Not all chains rattle.
Some speak in a gentle tone.

Kyra didn't stay bound because she was weak.
She stayed bound because Rose's voice sounded like the truth.
It felt like protection.
Like preparation.
But it was just polished fear—dressed up as wisdom.

You've heard that voice too, haven't you?

"God can't use you yet."
"You're too broken."
"You're not worthy of the call."

She didn't wait for the voice to go silent.
She moved while it was still speaking.
And that's where her power was born.

She stepped backstage at Fashion Week.
Even while doubt was still in her pocket, she:
Stopped apologizing for her accomplishments.
Refused to shrink in rooms she was called to fill.
Replaced fear-laced thoughts with God-breathed truth.
Started questioning the voice instead of agreeing with it.
Took the risk to move forward without waiting for full confidence.
Choose clarity over perfection.
And trusted obedience more than her feelings.

This was the turning point.

Kimberely R. Allen

The lie had a name—so did the truth that dismantled it.

The voice kept speaking, but she no longer bowed to it.
Its power faded as she moved in truth.
She advanced while it clung to the old script.
It didn't disappear all at once—
but its grip loosened the moment she stopped answering.
The moment she chose to believe something greater.

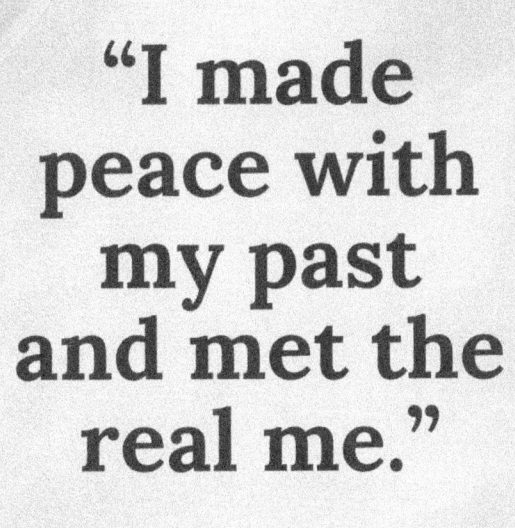

"I made peace with my past and met the real me."

- Kimberely R. Allen

Reflection:

The loudest voice in your mind is often the one that has lived there the longest. But that doesn't mean it belongs there.

Ask yourself:

- What voice do I trust more than God's?
- What truth have you been too afraid to believe?
- How would your life shift if you trusted God's voice more than your inner critic?

Silencing shame starts with questioning it.

You don't need the voice to stop before you start walking.
You just need to stop letting it lead.

Please use the space below to record your thoughts:

_____

_____

_____

_____

_____

_____

_____

_____

_____

_____

_____

_____

_____

_____

_____

_____

_____

---

* * *

"I once listened to the voice that questioned my worth. But now, I hear a greater one—soft yet strong—reminding me: I am more than enough."

Chapter 4

I Refuse to Keep Waiting at the Window

She said she'd be back.

Kyra remembered it.
Not the date.
Not the weather.
Not even what her mother wore.
But the words?
Etched in her bones.
Branded in memory.

"I'll be back for you."

She didn't cry.
Didn't plead.
She simply nodded,
like a child who still believed
that promises had weight.

And so she waited.

One day.
One week.
Then a lifetime wrapped in questions.

Why didn't she come back?

The waiting built walls inside her—
quiet ones, the kind you don't see until someone leans in.
And with every passing year,
those walls declared the same thing:
"People leave.
Even the ones who say they won't.
Especially the ones who say they love you."

Rose didn't need to shout.
She lived in the absence of sound.
She mocked her in every unanswered phone call,
every birthday candle unlit,
every dream tucked too tightly beneath disappointment.

"See? You're forgettable."
"You weren't worth coming back for."

And Kyra believed her.
Not because she wanted to.
But because no one else was speaking louder.

Somewhere between childhood and womanhood,
she stopped going to the window.
But the ache never left.
It just curled itself inside her ribcage
and waited for a quiet night to stretch out again.

At twenty, she got the call.
Her mother had died.
No goodbye.

No last hug.
No explanation.

Just an unfinished story,
sealed.

She wasn't a little girl anymore.
But the little girl in her still asked:
"Did she try?"
"Was I enough to come back for?"
"Was I ever enough at all?"

Kyra learned to smile with grace
and love with boundaries.
She dressed her hurt in kindness.
Softened her edges with hospitality.
But let no one close enough
to see the glass behind the grin.

Friendships were earned through silent tests.
Unspoken riddles.
Invisible hoops no one knew they were jumping through.

And when they failed—
because people always fail when the test is secret—
Abandonment slipped through the cracks.

Not like a scream.
More like a sigh.

"Do you hear that?" said Rose.
"That's the sound of them leaving."
"You've always been the extra line in a story that didn't need you."
"Too much to love. Not enough to keep."

She believed it sometimes.

Her scars were layered.
And grief doesn't always knock before it enters.

She told herself solitude was all she needed.
That independence was nobility.
That she liked being alone.

But the truth?

She hated it.

Not all the time.
Just when it felt like the aftersound of people who didn't stay.

What people didn't know—
not even the man who loved her—
was that when they weren't under the same roof,
when he was in one house
and she was in another,
the quiet didn't comfort her.
It lingered on.

Abandonment didn't knock.
It slipped in unnoticed,
wearing new clothes.
Familiar voice.
New disguise.

It didn't shout.
It didn't slam doors.
It simply said, again:

"See? You're always the one they're willing to live without."

She never said it aloud.
Not to him.

Not to anyone.

Not because she didn't feel it—
but because she didn't want to sound fragile.
Didn't want to be labeled dramatic.
Didn't want pity.

She had survived worse.
She had stitched herself back together with silence.

But even grown women
who know how to survive
still carry the little girl
who waited too long at the window.

Her sisters, her friends—
they didn't know this part.
They'd tease her, gently, when it was time to go:

"You don't really want us to leave, do you?"

And they were right.

She didn't.

Kyra would stretch the visit,
stretch the stories,
stretch the warmth—
offering blankets, snacks, conversation,
anything to slow the goodbye.

But what puzzled her most
was how different it felt
when the roles were reversed.

She didn't like staying overnight.

Didn't like settling into someone else's space.

She trusted her home.
Her walls.
Her bed.

But not theirs.

Because in someone else's world,
you could be asked to leave.

And that—
that felt too much
like being left
all over again.

She didn't realize how deep it ran—
not until one quiet night
when the house sat still
and the silence settled heavy.

She sat at the edge of the bed,
feet brushing the floor,
hands resting in her lap,
breath caught somewhere between sigh and sob.

The TV was off.
The clock ticked too loud.
And the silence?
It wrapped around her shoulders
like a blanket she never asked for.

Her phone lay beside her—
fully charged, untouched.
No calls.
No visitors.

No noise.

Her husband was at the church,
preparing the Word,
decluttering another house,
assuming—like everyone else—
that she was fine being alone.

But she wasn't angry.
She had never told him otherwise.
She had never told anyone.

She had just gotten used to
making solitude look holy.
Making silence look strong.

Until now.

She sighed—
not deeply,
just enough to feel it.

And in a voice that barely left her lips,
she spoke softly,
"I don't like this."

Not the quiet.
Not the stillness.
Not the murmuring of her own thoughts
in a room full of furniture
but empty of presence.

For the first time,
she didn't judge herself for it.
Didn't label it needy.
Didn't bury it beneath prayer or performance.

She simply allowed the ache to speak:

"I don't want people to leave.
Not because I'm weak.
But because too many already have."

She picked up her journal—
not to write something deep,
just something real.
Something honest.

The ink bled fast,
hurried strokes across paper
like a heart too full to pace itself:

> *I like being surrounded by people.*
> *I don't like when they leave.*
> *I'm not needy—*
> *I just remember what it felt like*
> *when no one came back.*
> *That scars that stayed with me.*
> *It settled in.*
> *And I still carry it.*
> *Even now,*
> *I don't always know how to feel safe*
> *when the house gets quiet.*
> *I wish someone would just sit here with me—*
> *not talk.*
> *Just be.*

That was it.
No edits. No metaphors.
Just truth.

She didn't analyze it.
Didn't wrap it in scripture or silence it with shame.

She closed the journal,
and for the first time in a long time—
she felt seen.

Not by the world.
Not by her friends.
Not even by the ones who loved her.

But by herself.

She didn't cry.
Not that night.
There were no trembling hands or
prayers shouted into pillows.
No grand healing moment
where the walls shook.

She just breathed.

A slow, deliberate breath—
like her lungs finally remembered
they were allowed to exhale.

She stood from the bed,
walked softly to the kitchen,
and scooped herself some ice cream.
Not to soothe.
Not to numb.
Just to care.

A small act of presence.

Then,
she turned on a light in the family room.
Not because she needed it to see—
but because sometimes,

when you've lived through abandonment,
leaving the light on
is how you remind yourself
you're still here.

She didn't fill the silence.
She didn't run from it.

She sat with it—
not as punishment,
but as a quiet declaration:

"I'm not alone.
I'm healing.
And I'm still here."

She didn't try to fill the silence.
She didn't run from it either.
She let it sit beside her,
like an old companion
she no longer needed to fear.

There, in that stillness,
the truth lagged behind—
that this ache, this loneliness,
was not hers alone to carry.

There were others.
Women who moved through the world
with grace in their step
but heaviness in their chest.
Women who stood in crowded rooms
yet still felt the steady sound of emptiness
rattle through their ribs.

Some had spouses—

but loneliness still crept in at night.
Some turned off lights
in apartments that reminded them of their prayers.
Some kept closets full of memories
and hearts full of questions
they never dared to ask aloud.

There were so many stories
written in the silence of furnished rooms—
stories of women
who had loved and lost,
who had waited and wondered,
who had whispered
"I don't want to be alone"
only in their minds
because the world had taught them
to dress longing as power
and silence as survival.

Kyra didn't know all their names.
She didn't have to.

She could feel them.

And perhaps,
somewhere beyond the walls of her own home,
God felt them, too.
The little girl still waiting at the window.
He saw every tear.
And He did not pass by.

He sat with her.
With her.

The one who still kept the lights on,
not out of fear—

but as a quiet reminder:
they were still here.

Still breathing.
Still healing.
Still rising.

And though the room felt quiet,
they were never truly alone.

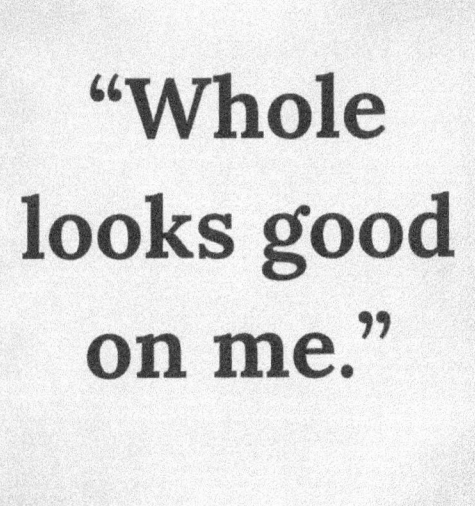

"Whole
looks good
on me."

- Kimberely R. Allen

Reflection:

Abandonment doesn't always show up in explosions. Sometimes it's displayed quietly in how we wait, how we love, how we hold back.

Ask yourself:

- What's the earliest memory you have of feeling forgotten or left behind?
- In what ways has that memory shaped how you form relationships now?
- What parts of yourself are still sitting by the window?

You are not too much for wanting presence.
You are not too little to be worth staying for.

Please use the space below to record your thoughts:

_____
_____
_____
_____
_____
_____
_____
_____
_____
_____
_____
_____
_____
_____
_____
_____
_____

_____
_____
_____
_____
_____
_____
_____
_____
_____
_____
_____
_____
_____
_____
_____
_____
_____
_____
_____
_____
_____
_____
_____
_____
_____
_____
_____
_____
_____
_____
_____
_____
_____

* * *

*"I may have been held by lies, but truth has come for me. Every day, I am
loosening the grip of the voice that tried to silence me."*

Chapter 5

I Am Breaking Free

She didn't break free beneath stained glass ceilings.
There was no altar call. No organ swell.
No tears streaming down like oil.
She broke free with scissors in her hand.

The dress?
Gone.
The one she wore when shame clung to her like skin.
She cut it apart like it still had hands.
Uninvited. Unwelcome.
Unworthy to stay.

She didn't pray first.
Didn't ask for counsel.
Didn't seek confirmation or cue.
She just did it.

Because sometimes deliverance doesn't come
through weeping or wailing,
but through a woman

finally choosing to stand.

She stopped wearing what bondage picked out for her.
She changed her number.
Deleted names she once released prayers over.
Unfollowed competition she never signed up for.
Stopped scrolling for proof of her own worth.

She quieted the gossip—not just with others,
but with herself.
No more replays of her lowest chapters.
No more mental marathons
with shame as the coach and fear on repeat.

She read books—
not just sugarcoated pages wrapped in pastel,
but words that sharpened her voice.
Strategy. Growth. Leadership. Truth.
She fed her mind the kind of truth
it had been starving to believe.

She joined a circle of women who knew her rhythm.
Pastors' wives, yes—
but not for prestige or platform.
For sisterhood.
For spaces where she didn't need to teach,
just breathe.
To say "me too" and hear it back.

She broke the cycle quietly.
No livestream. No announcement.
Just obedience in motion.
A private revolution.

She stopped waiting for apologies.
Stopped bending to fit rooms

that shrunk her radiance.
She made room for rest—
without explanation.
Because rest is holy too.

She stopped asking,
"What if I fail?"
and started declaring,
"But what if I don't?"

And with every move—
every cut,
every boundary,
every no that honored her yes—
Rose's voice began to fade.

Freedom wasn't just a dream
or a distant destination.
It was a fight.

And this time—
she was winning.

Reflection:

Freedom rarely comes with a crowd. It starts quietly—like a woman speaking to herself, "Not anymore."

Ask yourself:

- What have you been carrying that was never yours to hold?
- Are there places or people that still hold the key to your healing?
- What's one belief, habit, or voice you're ready to release today?

Freedom is not about perfection—it's about movement.
Every step you take toward your recovery matters.

Please use the space below to record your thoughts:

_____
_____
_____
_____
_____
_____
_____
_____
_____
_____
_____
_____
_____
_____
_____

_____
_____
_____
_____
_____
_____
_____
_____
_____
_____
_____
_____
_____
_____
_____
_____
_____
_____
_____
_____
_____
_____
_____
_____
_____
_____
_____
_____
_____

* * *

"Every step I take toward freedom is sacred. I am no longer shrinking. I am rising, unchained, and unbecoming everything I was never meant to carry."

Chapter 6

I Carried Grace Through the Fire

Growth didn't come all at once.
It came in fragments—
in the quiet spaces where pride had to be put down,
and grace had to rise in its place.
In the stretching.
The sifting.
The slow refining by God's steady hand.

Kyra had lived through storms,
but it was the everyday moments that tested her most.
Moments where grace wasn't a feeling—
it was a decision.
A choice to be still when the old her wanted to roar.

Three encounters etched themselves into her memory.
Not dramatic. Not grand.
But holy in the way only growth could be.
Blessed,
because they cost her something.

There was the grocery store,
where grace had to stand tall under the weight of old assumptions.

Then the nail shop,
where small talk turned sharp without warning—
and misunderstanding slipped in between polish and pause.
Grace had to stay seated,
unbothered and unbent,
while her silence dried under fluorescent lights.

And finally, Tamara.
The unexpected encounter
that taught her strength didn't always speak—
sometimes, it simply stayed silent
and let God defend.

Each moment stitched a new layer into her soul.
Each one uttered the same truth:
"My grace is sufficient for you,
for My power is made perfect in weakness."
(2 Corinthians 12:9)

This was what growth looked like for her now.
Not applause.
Not recognition.
But the unseen victories
where grace led the way,
and silence became strength.

The first encounter came in aisle seven.

Kyra had only come for almond milk, eggs,
maybe something sweet to chase the week away.
But restoration rarely checks your calendar.
It simply arrives—uninvited, unavoidable.

She turned the corner,
and there it was—her name,
spoken like it still belonged to a girl she no longer was.

"Girl, is that you?"

The voice hit first.
Then the face followed.
Sonya James.

Grin wide.
Eyes knowing.
That same laugh that once roamed through hallways
lined with whispers and warnings.

"Wow, Kyra. You look different,
but I bet you ain't changed one bit."

The words dripped with nostalgia,
but landed with weight.

Still got that mischievous look.

Still, as if she had stayed the same.
Still, as if growth hadn't taken root.
Still, as if time hadn't demanded its price.

And just like that,
the past rushed in like a wave she hadn't braced for.

The urge to explain,
to list her growth like a résumé—
I'm married now.
I serve at the church.
I've healed,
I've changed—

but grace kept her still.

This wasn't a moment for defense.
It was a moment for discernment.

Kyra smiled, soft and short.
Not cold, but not open either.

Some memories didn't need revival.
Some names didn't need an invitation.

It wasn't loud.
There were no tears.
Just grace—quiet, grown,
and uninterested in proving anything.

But as the weight of old wounds pressed against her soul,
Kyra did not fold.
She stood still—
not in fear,
but in remembrance.

She closed her eyes for just a moment,
long enough to gather grace.
Long enough to remind herself:
She was not that girl anymore.

Not the runner.
Not the rebel.
Not the sound of someone else's wound.

She had been rewritten.

A new creation,
born from fire and faith,
refined by grace.

She exhaled slowly,
let the breath carry out what didn't belong.
Then opened her eyes—clear, steady.

Her smile met Sonya's grin with calm resolve.
"Sonya, I promise you…
I'm not the same teenager I used to be."

Sonya blinked—
surprised, maybe even unsure.
And then she laughed.
"Okay, okay! I hear you!"

But this wasn't small talk anymore.
This was testimony wrapped in casual tone.

Kyra didn't flinch.
Her voice didn't waver.
She let the truth sit in the air,
Bold and full of weight.

"For real though… I've grown.
Life changed me.
God changed me.
So if we're going to talk—
let's talk about now."

The situation shifted.
Sonya's eyes softened,
her smirk gave way to sincerity.

She studied Kyra like she hadn't really seen her before.
Not until now.

"Alright then," she said,
with a nod that felt more like a bow.

"What have you been up to?"

And just like that,
grace held the room.

Not because Kyra needed to prove she had changed—
but because she no longer needed permission
to be who she had become.

In that moment,
Kyra realized—
this wasn't about old words or shared memories.
This was about being a witness.
About what it meant to live the change,
not just speak of it.

She didn't need to defend who she had become.
She simply was.

Grace had become her boundary.
Strength had become her posture.
And the past?
It no longer held the pen.

She didn't flinch.
Didn't fluster.
Didn't fold into who she used to be.

Sonya's words,
though laced with history,
fell soft against the woman she was now.

Like water over stone.
Unmoved.
Unchanged by the sound.

The Little Girl Within

Because when you know who you are in Christ,
you stop explaining what you're not.

Kyra's silence wasn't empty—
it was loud with dignity.
Laced with discernment.
Rooted in redemption.

She would no longer entertain conversations
that tried to drag her back
into names she no longer answered to.

She had stopped chasing closure.
She no longer needed to correct every false perception.

Her identity was secure.
Not in Sonya's memory.
Not in her reputation.
But in the One who had rewritten her story.

She didn't have to prove her growth.
She walked in it.

And that—
was more than enough.

The second encounter came quietly,
wrapped not in memory,
but in acetone and soft music
humming through ceiling speakers.

The scent of polish floated in the air
as Kyra rested her hands in warm water,
letting silence stretch over her like a towel
pulled fresh from the dryer.

It was supposed to be a moment of peace—
a simple fill,
a break from the weight of ministry and memory.

But peace was interrupted
by a presence she felt before she saw.

Sister Geraldine.

Her voice cut through the soft hum of the nail files,
sweet like sugar—
but sharp at the edges.

"Well, look at you," she said,
sliding into the chair beside her.
"I was just talking about you the other day."

Kyra looked up slowly,
a polite smile forming,
even as her stomach braced
for what she already knew was coming.

"You know,
I remember when you used to be up in that choir stand,
singing like an angel on Sundays…
But whew—Saturday nights?"
Geraldine leaned in,
her voice dipped in nostalgia and judgment.

"Y'all had the neighborhood buzzing.
We heard it all—
the sneaking, the drinking,
the smoke clouding up your witness."

She laughed,
softly,

knowingly.

"And now you're what? A preacher?"

The words spread like fumes—
filling the space with insinuation.

The weight of her words came crashing in—
not like a storm,
but like an old, familiar ache
pressing against a healed scar.

But Kyra didn't flinch.
She didn't crumble.
Didn't fold.
Didn't explain.

She inhaled grace,
anchoring herself in the peace she now wore like armor.

She let her silence speak.
Let her poise preach.
Let grace do what rebuttals could not.

Her hands, still soaking,
were no longer symbols of guilt
but of cleansing.

She didn't rush to defend her past—
because God had already covered it.

What Geraldine remembered was real.
But it was no longer relevant.

Growth doesn't need permission
from those who watched you fall

to validate your rise.

So Kyra stayed seated,
upright,
spine straight,
polish drying
as grace held her still.

She had nothing to prove.
Only God's light to carry.
And the older woman's words,
meant to sting,
only confirmed what heaven already knew:

She was not who she used to be.
And grace looked good on her.

"Yes," she said, her voice even,
gentle—
but firm.
"I did all of that.
And still, God had a plan for me."

No heat in her tone.
No edge.
Just truth—softened by time
and solidified by transformation.

"I know people talked,"
she continued,
her words steady as a river finding its path.
"I know they judged what they never understood.
But what they didn't see…
was the pain behind the rebellion.
The girl trying to escape.
The girl reaching for God

but not knowing how to call His name."

She looked up,
her eyes clear.

"But He saw me.
And He never let go."

She didn't argue.
Didn't defend.
Didn't return insult for injury.

She testified.

Letting her growth speak for itself.
Letting her wholeness fill the room
without saying another word.

The air shifted.

Geraldine's brows furrowed—
not in judgment now,
but in something like quiet reckoning.

"Well," she said, after a moment,
"I suppose we all have a past."

Kyra's smile was soft.
Not smug.
Not sharp.
Just… sure.

"We do.
The difference is,
I don't live in mine anymore."

A silence followed—
but it wasn't uncomfortable.
It was intentional.
The kind of pause
where the past nods respectfully to the present
before stepping aside.

She didn't need Geraldine's approval.
Didn't need the room to clap.
Redemption doesn't beg to be believed.
It just stands—
evident.
Alive.
Unshaken.

And then came the third encounter,
the one she didn't see coming

Rejection had always walked a step behind her—
never loud,
never far.

It tarried in doorways,
hid behind affirmations,
and shadowed even the best of days.

Kyra knew its name well.
Knew how it sounded in her father's silence.
How it echoed in sideways glances.
How it stitched itself into moments that should have felt safe.

But she also knew this truth:
she hadn't always been innocent in her ache.
Yes—she had been mistreated.
Dismissed.
Forgotten.

But trauma, when it sits too long,
becomes sharp.
And Kyra had learned how to cut before being cut.

She used sarcasm like a sword.
Silence like a wall.
And pride like perfume—
strong enough to mask the bruises underneath.

Because when rejection becomes your teacher,
sometimes you mimic its lessons
just to feel like you're the one writing the script.

She didn't bully to be cruel.
She bullied to be seen.
To matter.
To win the war of invisibility.

And then came Tamara.

She hadn't expected to see her.
Not here.
Not now.
But there she was—
a walking memory of the past
wearing the same name and holding the same gaze.

Tamara didn't flinch.
Didn't smile.
Didn't pretend to forget.

She looked at Kyra
like the hurt had never passed.
Like time hadn't healed.
Like she was still the villain in someone else's story.

And maybe,
in Tamara's story,
she was.

Back then, Kyra had mocked her tears.
Used words as daggers.
Withheld kindness like it was currency.
And all the while,
she was just a girl with her own wounds—
bleeding on people who didn't cause them.

But that didn't excuse it.
Not today.

Tamara's voice was clipped.
Her tone cool.
A defense built from years of silence.

Kyra felt the sting.
She didn't run from it.
Didn't meet dagger with dagger.
Didn't reach for pride to cover her shame.

Grace surfaced instead.

She stepped forward—
not in defense,
but in surrender.

Her voice, steady.
Soft, but sure.

Tamara, I said—steady but soft,
"You don't have to smile.
You don't have to be okay with me.
But I need to say this anyway…"

The words fell like water
on soil that had been dry too long.

She didn't stop me.
Didn't interrupt.
Didn't offer grace—
but she gave me space.
And that was enough.

So, I kept going.

"I remember who I was back then.
The sharpness.
The stares.
The sarcasm.
I remember the way I used my mouth like a sword—
cutting to be seen,
to be strong,
to survive."

It wasn't a full circle.
It wasn't a restoration.

But it was a seed.
And sometimes,
grace plants what pride can never grow.

Her arms stayed folded,
her jaw stayed tight,
but I didn't turn away.
So, I kept going.

"I don't expect you to forget.
I wouldn't ask you to.
But I need you to know—
I'm not that girl anymore.

God got to me.
He broke the hardness.
He untaught me what misery had trained me to do.

And whether or not you ever see me differently,
I just needed to say this out loud:

You didn't deserve any of it.
The ridicule.
The rejection.
The weight of wounds that were never yours to carry.

I see that now.
And I'm sorry."

The air hung heavy.
Her silence louder than any reply.
So Kyra asked,
"Can I pray for you?"

No answer came.
But she didn't need permission
to release restoration into the atmosphere.

She closed her eyes,
not to escape,
but to stand in the gap.

"God," she declared,
"Let me be a mirror of You—
for the version of her I mocked,
for the beauty I refused to see.

Restore what I tried to steal.
Heal what I helped hurt.
Remind her she's more than anyone's memory.

Let grace find her today,
even if it doesn't come from me."

In Jesus' Name.
Amen.

When her eyes opened,
Tamara hadn't moved.
But Kyra had.

From guilt to growth.
From shame to strength.
From cruelty to compassion.

Grace didn't erase the past—
but it rewrote the present.
And even if forgiveness never came,
Kyra knew she would keep showing up with grace,
because she remembered how desperately she once needed it too.

She'd spent years walking into rooms
where her past arrived before her name.
Where old mistakes spoke louder than her rebirth ever could.
But grace?
Grace reached in both directions—
to the wound and to the one who caused it.

It found the girl with regret on her lips
and the girl with torment behind her eyes.
It stood between them like a bridge,
steady and still.

Grace didn't make the memory disappear.
But it reclaimed the moment.

It stood tall in rooms full of reminders.

It spoke softly in places where silence once screamed.
And it declared a truth Kyra now carried like a mantle:

She was not her worst moment.
She was not someone else's version of who she used to be.
She was *grace in motion*.

And if God could extend it to her—
then surely, it could flow through her, too.

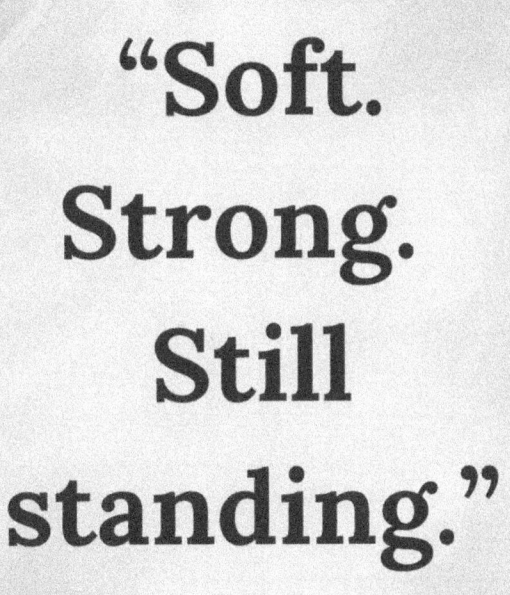

"Soft. Strong. Still standing."

– Kimberely R. Allen

Reflection:

Sometimes we think grace will pull us out of the fire—but often, it's what holds us together in it.

Ask yourself:

- Have you confused being "pressed" with being punished?
- Where have you seen grace show up when you least expected it?
- What has God preserved in you—even while you were being tested?

You don't have to look unshaken to be full of grace.
Sometimes, survival is the evidence of grace.

Please use the space below to record your thoughts:

_____

_____

_____

_____

_____

_____

_____

_____

_____

_____

_____

_____

_____

_____

_____

_____

* * *

"The flames didn't consume me. They revealed me. Grace stood firm while the fire reshaped me and I became."

Chapter 7

I Chose Surrender Over Striving

In the beginning, surrender was a stranger—
foreign, unwelcome, and cloaked in fear.

To Kyra, it didn't look like recovery.
It looked like weakness.
Not peace, but loss.
Not rest, but ruin.

Letting go felt like disappearing,
to lay down her shield and step into the unknown,
vulnerable and bare.

Heartbreak had trained her to grip tightly.
Every betrayal carved a message in her bones:
Don't let go. Don't trust. Don't fall.

She believed that control kept her safe,
that walls kept her from breaking.

To surrender?

That meant risking it all.
Her identity.
Her voice.
Her worth.

And if she let it all go—
who would she be without the challenges that made her?
For Kyra,
surrender didn't feel like freedom.
It felt like falling—
a quiet collapse beneath the weight of everything she feared.

It wasn't a gentle release.
It was the memory of defeat,
the terror of disappearing into the very heartache
she'd spent her whole life outrunning.

So she held on—
to habits that hardened her,
to patterns that punished her,
to fragments of control that frayed at the edges
but felt safer than the unknown.

She didn't know yet
that surrender wasn't her ending.

It was the door to her beginning.

Kyra once believed
that surrender would strip her down to shame—
naked, not in body,
but in truth.

She feared that if people really knew…
that she never finished school,
wasn't as sharp as they assumed,

started drinking at twelve,
had a child before marriage,
and gave her body away
when all she really wanted
was to feel seen—

They would never see her as worth too much.
Not grace.
Not love.
Certainly not God.

In her mind, surrender didn't sound like freedom.
It sounded like exposure.
Like stepping into the light
only to hand the world
more reasons to crucify her.

But what she didn't know then—
what unmerited love was gently whispering—
was this:

Surrender isn't about proving your worth.
It's about trusting
that God already called you worthy.
Even with your past.
Especially with your past.

She learned that lesson the hard way—
when she and her husband planted their first church,
and the title came wrapped in expectation:
First Lady.
Pastor's Wife.
The Woman Beside the Man of God.

It sounded honorable.
But felt heavy.

And then came the moment—
the one she'd never forget.

The Spirit stirred within her,
calling her to start
The First Lady's Women's Circle
Not just to host it.
But to lead it.
And not just to lead—
but to reveal.

To stand not as a picture of perfection,
but as a portrait of grace in progress.

She pleaded with God.
And told Him,
"I'm not that girl anymore.
I can't bleed here.
Not in front of them.
I carry a title now.
I've earned dignity.
Can't I serve them without uncovering myself?"

She thought the platform gave her permission to hide.
To drape herself in redemption
without ever undressing her truth.
To stand clothed in victory
but untouched by vulnerability.

She didn't yet understand
that redemption doesn't come from hiding.
And titles don't make you whole.
Truth does.

But God didn't let her off the hook.
And deep down, she knew why.

So, one trembling day,
with a heart full of questions
and a mouth full of truth,
she obeyed.

She told her story—
not all at once,
but enough to crack the silence,
enough to break something open,
enough to set something—or someone—free.

Not just in the room,
but in the spirit.
Not just for them,
but for her.

That day, she learned
surrender isn't weakness—
it's worship.
It's transparency wrapped in trust.
It's saying, "God, You can use this, too."

Even the parts she wanted to bury.
Even the pieces she thought disqualified her.
Even the chapters she once wished to erase.

As she looked around the room
and saw eyes filled with tears—
not pity,
but understanding—
something inside her began to shift.

The shame she wore like a covering
started to peel,
not because they all approved,
but because she finally stopped hiding.

Later that night,
Rose crept in—
the voice that had torched her for years,
the one who lied saying,
"You're not enough,"
"They see you as less,"
"You'll never be more than your past."

But this time,
Rose didn't roar.
She watched quietly
as Kyra sat alone with God,
still trembling
but not breaking.

A gentle nudge surfaced in her spirit,
soft and sacred:

"Transparency is painful, Lord… but it's helping me.
And I think it's blessing them, too."

She didn't need a polished past to lead women.
She just needed the courage
to stop pretending she never bled.

But that moment
didn't mean the struggle ended.

Over the years,
transparency still came
with trembling hands
and sweaty palms.

Every time God nudged her
to share that part of her story—
the one still tender,

the one she'd stitched closed with silence—
she felt the war rise again.

And Rose was never far.
Whispering like smoke curling through a crack:
"You said enough."
"They don't need to know that."
"You'll lose respect."
"You've already proven who you are now—
why go back?"

And sometimes,
Kyra wanted to believe her.
Because silence is safe.
And safety feels like control.

But deep down,
she knew better.

Because surrender
wasn't a one-time act at the altar—
it was a lifestyle.
A daily laying down.
A divine offering of truth
for the sake of being mended—
hers and theirs.

So she kept telling the truth.
Before strangers.
Before sisters.
Before rooms of women
who sat silent—
until her story
gave them permission
to speak their own.

Because no matter
how loud Rose got,
Kyra had already decided:

I will not be quiet
when God tells me to speak.

I may tremble,
I may weep,
I may walk in afraid—
but I will not withhold
what healed me.

And that—
that was power.

Not the kind that comes
from being polished or perfect,
but the kind birthed
in obedience.
The kind that breaks chains
The kind that turns surrender
into strength.

But as Kyra journeyed deeper into restoration,
the meaning of surrender began to shift.
Not quickly.
Not cleanly.
It came like dawn—
slow and soft,
stretching over the dark places
she once kept locked tight.

Surrender, she learned,
wasn't about giving up.
It wasn't weakness.

The Little Girl Within

It wasn't defeat.

It was a holy release—
a letting go of what had held her hostage
in the name of survival.

Through sessions with Dr. Yates,
gentle counsel and honest reflection,
through whispered prayers and quiet breakthroughs,
she began to see it clearly:

Surrender wasn't about losing control.
It was about trusting God
to hold the pieces
she no longer had the strength to carry.

It was in the quiet moments—
misery sitting beside her like an old friend—
that surrender started to look different.

Not like weakness,
but like courage.

Not giving up,
but letting go.

She began to believe
that maybe restoration wasn't found in holding it all together—
but in letting God hold her.

In those still spaces,
with tears that didn't demand answers
and faith that whispered "still, I trust You,"
she started to see it clearly:

Surrender wasn't passive.

It wasn't silence or resignation.
It was participation.
A divine exchange—
laying down the burden
so that redemption could rise in its place

Just like the Holy Scripture declares,
To appoint unto them that mourn in Zion,
to give unto them beauty for ashes,
the oil of joy for mourning,
the garment of praise for the spirit of heaviness;
that they might be called trees of righteousness,
the planting of the Lord,
that he might be glorified.
(Isaiah 61:3)

It was an act of boldness,
to hand God the weight of what she'd carried for too long,
and trust Him
to make something holy out of the heaviness.

By the end of her journey,
surrender no longer looked like defeat—
it looked like freedom.

What once felt like losing control
became the clearest path to reclaiming her identity.
It wasn't the end.
It was the beginning.
The door that opened when her hands finally let go.

She didn't disappear in the letting go—
she discovered herself.
In surrender, she found her sound again.
Her softness.
Her strength.

It was the quiet courage to trust God
with the parts of her story that still stung.
To stop carrying what wasn't hers to hold.
To believe that renewal could be holy
even when it came in pieces.

Kyra's life became a living testimony:
Surrender is not weakness.
It is the soil where wholeness grows.
It is the act of saying,
"God, I trust You more than I trust my fear."

And as Kyra stepped fully into her renewal,
her life became a quiet whisper to the world around her—
a testimony that the weight of the past
was never meant to be carried forever.

She had let go.
She had leaned in.
And in that release,
she discovered a strength that had always been waiting.
A freedom that lived just beyond the fear.

The kind of freedom
that only surrender could unlock.

And when Kyra stood there—
not perfect, but whole,
not fearless, but full—
she didn't just feel healed.

She felt ready.

Ready to live fully.
To lead boldly.
To love freely.

Kimberely R. Allen

To be the woman God always knew she was.

Because surrender hadn't silenced her.
It had saved her.

And in that consecrated surrender,
she emerged.

There is a restoration so sacred,
it only begins when the hiding ends.
Transparency, she learned,
was never weakness—
it was the quiet revolution her soul had longed for.

With every truth she allowed to rise,
shame lost its grip.
The enemy's whispers lost their power.
And something holy broke open
in the spaces she once tried to seal shut.

For years, Kyra had guarded the chapters
that felt too unworthy to share.
But in time,
she began to sense that the very places
she thought disqualified her
were the ones God was reaching for—
not just to heal her,
but to free someone else through her story.

So she wrote.
She wrestled with the weight of it.
She sat in the silence of surrender,
and asked God to reveal the healing
hidden in her honesty.

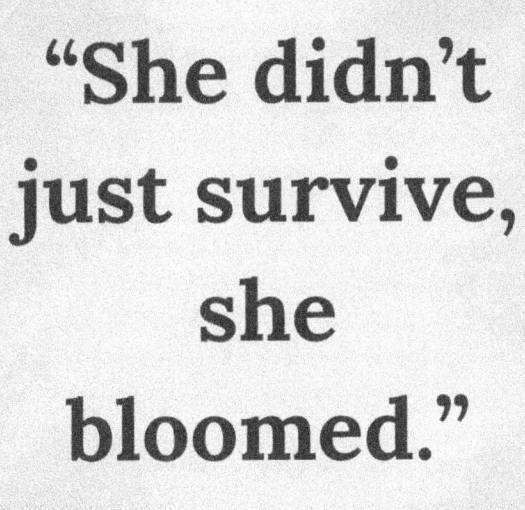

"She didn't just survive, she bloomed."

- Kimberely R. Allen

Reflection:

True surrender doesn't mean you've given up. It means you've finally laid it down—so God can pick it up.

Ask yourself:

- What are you still holding on to because it gives you a false sense of control?
- Has your need to "manage" your hurt kept you from fully being restored?
- What might God be waiting to place in your hands if you'd let go of what's in them now?

Surrender isn't weakness.
It's choosing to trade your burden for God's peace.

Please use the space below to record your thoughts:

_____

_____

_____

_____

_____

_____

_____

_____

_____

_____

_____

_____

_____

_____

_____

_____

---

* * *

*"I don't lose when I let go—I win peace, I win clarity, I win me.
In surrender, I am not giving up—I am giving it to God."*

Chapter 8

I Stand with Unshakable Confidence

Confidence was never the absence of fear.
It wasn't the loudest voice in the room
or the absence of trembling hands.
It was quiet—anchored.
The kind of strength that whispers in the storm:
I know who I am, even if you don't.

For Kyra, that kind of confidence didn't arrive overnight.
It was cultivated—
not from applause, or titles,
but in the quiet corners where God reminded her:
"You are already enough, simply because I say so."

It was no longer about perfection.
No longer about proving.
Confidence had become a posture—
a way of standing, even when shaking.
A way of walking forward,
not because every step was certain,

but because she had finally learned
Who walked with her.

And when identity is rooted in Christ,
no shifting opinion,
no image of the past,
no shadow of the unknown—
can shake what's been secured by grace.

Kyra had always carried herself with grace and style,
but there was a time when every outfit was like protection.
Her fashion was flair— but it was also camouflage.
She dressed to disappear,
to blend in,
to meet expectations she never agreed to.
Each piece chosen not to express,
but to suppress—
to quiet the parts of her that dared to shine.

She dimmed her light on purpose,
fearing that if she ever stepped out fully,
she would be "too much"
for a world that had only ever asked her to be less.

But unshakable confidence isn't stitched into fabric—
it's woven into identity.
It doesn't rise from what you wear,
but from who you are
when the layers are stripped away.

It took time.
It took truth.
It took tears.
For Kyra to understand:
Hiding was not humility.

And dimming her light
was never protection—
it was self-erasure wrapped in fear.

She had spent years
shrinking to avoid rejection,
blending to avoid being misunderstood.
But God hadn't called her to disappear.
He was calling her to stand out—
not for hand claps,
but for assignment.

Confidence, she learned,
was never found in the mirror's reflection—
but in the still, divine whisper of God:
You are enough.
I made you enough.

But this time was different.
The next time Kyra walked into a family gathering,
she didn't shrink to fit the corners of the room.
Something had changed.

She entered, not as the woman who once feared their glances,
but as the one who had made peace with her reflection.
She no longer wore invisibility like a cloak.
She stood—rooted, radiant, real.

It wasn't just her outfit that turned heads,
but the confidence that clothed her.
Shoulders back.
Head lifted.
She moved with quiet power,
like every step was a declaration:
I am no longer who I used to be.

The layers of doubt, shame, and insecurity
no longer held her hostage—
they had fallen off like old skin.
And what remained
was someone whole.

Some noticed.
Others couldn't quite name it,
but they felt the shift.
The same relatives who once whispered her name like a
warning
now looked at her with quiet curiosity—
maybe even respect.

But Kyra wasn't walking in to prove anything.
That was the difference.

Her confidence wasn't loud.
It didn't need to be.
It was settled. Rooted. Still.

She no longer sought validation to feel valuable.
The woman who once dressed to disappear
was now clothed in conviction.

And for the first time,
she didn't just appear to belong—
she knew she did.

She had come to understand something critical:
Her worth was never up for debate.
It didn't live in glances,
or side comments,
or family expectations.

She no longer had to fold herself small

to make others feel big.
She no longer had to retreat to be respected.
The weight of their opinions—
the old pressure to play invisible—
had lost its grip.

This time,
she showed up whole.
Fully.
Unapologetically.
Unshrinkable.

Because true confidence
isn't arrogance.
It's an agreement.
A quiet yes to God about who you are.

Her past entanglement with hesitation?
She let it go.
She wasn't waiting for permission anymore.

As the evening unfolded,
a cousin she hadn't spoken to in years pulled her aside.
There was no small talk,
just a long, searching gaze
before the words finally came out.

"You look… different,"
she said softly, almost reverently.
"Not just your clothes or your hair.
It's something else.
You seem… whole.
Like you're comfortable in your own skin."

Kyra smiled—
not with pride,

but with peace.

"I am," she said,
her voice steady.
"It took me a long time to get here.
But I'm finally here."

And that was it.
No claps.
No announcement.
Just an undeniable recognition.
A quiet confirmation
that rebirth had taken root,
that confidence had replaced camouflage.

This wasn't performance.
It was presence.
She wasn't trying to be seen—
she simply was.

Fully.
Boldly.
Unapologetically.

However, that beautiful moment didn't linger long.

She stepped into the larger room—
Where the residue of laughter remained,
and familiar faces filled the space.
But so did the familiar remarks.

"Why do you always dress so extra?"
Her family.
Her friends.
Their voices dripped with that old cocktail—
a blend of curiosity and quiet criticism.

Smirks masked as jokes.
Comments wrapped in concern.

And for a moment,
Kyra heard it—
the old voice rising from within,
the one that used to make her shrink,
the one that once convinced her
she had to tone herself down to be tolerated.

She remembered those days.
The ones when she'd bite her lip
just to keep from crying.
When she'd retreat into corners,
folding herself into silence
just to avoid the sting of being misunderstood.

But not today.

Not after that powerful moment with her cousin.
Not after the years it took to build this kind of peace.
The words tried to find a wound,
but there were no open wounds left to pierce.

Her heart beat faster,
but not from fear.
It was anticipation—
the deep knowing of who she had become,
and the joy that now lived in her bones.

She didn't flinch.
She didn't shrink.
She didn't perform.
Because today,
she didn't need the room's approval to feel worthy of it.

Kimberely R. Allen

She stood there—
still,
soft,
settled.

She had nothing to prove.
She was not molded by their memory of her.
She was anchored in her unshakable confidence.

Her presence was a testament to the power of
surrender,
healing—
embracing who God had created her to be.

No longer defined by her past
or her family's expectations,
Kyra had finally stepped into the fullness
of who she was always meant to be—
a woman unafraid to be herself and confident.

And as she sat at the table,
surrounded by the same faces
that once made her feel small,
Kyra felt something unfamiliar…
Empowered.

There was no tightness in her body,
no silent plea for belonging,
no invisible weight pressing her into the margins.

She had already taken her seat—
not just at the table,
but in the fullness of her life.

Her calm was no longer mistaken for passivity.
It was bold.

Her stillness— no longer rooted in fear.
It was fortified.

She no longer needed to raise her voice to be heard.
She spoke when led.
She stood when necessary.
And when she sat—
she did so in the fullness of her own becoming.

The family couldn't quite name what had changed.
But they felt it.
They had witnessed the shift.
A woman once fragile with fear
now grounded in her own power.

Not defiant.
Not demanding.
Just… whole.

They may never fully understand her journey.
But the miracle wasn't in their comprehension—
it was in her release.

She no longer waited for them to get it.
She no longer adjusted herself to be digestible.
She no longer measured her worth by their reactions.

Kyra had stopped waiting to be chosen.
She had chosen herself.

And in that deliberate choosing,
she became unshakable.

Her confidence didn't glitter—
it glowed.
It didn't shout—

it stood.
It didn't crave the spotlight—
it carried the weight of fire survived
and freedom found.

A quiet roar wrapped in grace—
that was the woman she had become.

"Unfolding.
Unashamed.
Unstoppable."

- Kimberely R. Allen

Reflection:

Real confidence isn't found in validation.
It's found in the quiet knowing that you're called, even when you don't feel qualified.

Ask yourself:

- Have you been waiting for others to confirm what God already told you?
- In what ways are you shrinking to fit into rooms you've already outgrown?
- What does it look like to walk boldly, even when you feel unsure?

Confidence isn't the absence of fear—it's the presence of faith in motion.

Please use the space below to record your thoughts:

_____
_____
_____
_____
_____
_____
_____
_____
_____
_____
_____
_____
_____
_____
_____
_____

---

* * *

*"My confidence is not in applause—it's in the quiet knowing that I am called,
seen, and strengthened by a God who never changes His mind about me."*

Chapter 9

I Am Finally Healed

Restoration didn't come the way Kyra imagined.
It wasn't wrapped in fireworks or grand displays.
Sometimes, it whispered through the quiet—
soft and subtle, like a breeze slipping under a door long closed.
Other times, it broke in like a storm—
unexpected, undeniable,
revealing that she'd traveled farther than she knew,
mended more than she thought.

But when rebirth truly took root,
something within her adjusted.
Not just the world around her—
but the very atmosphere of her soul.

Her voice carried a new grace.
Her shoulders stood taller,
no longer bowed under invisible burdens.
The chaos that once felt familiar became foreign.
She stopped folding herself to fit into places too small.
She breathed deeper.

Moved freer.
Loved fuller.

She had waited so long—
wondering if renewal would ever reach her,
if peace could grow in soil once saturated with pain.

She no longer prayed for miracles.
She just wanted breath without burden,
days that didn't ache.
And somehow, in the ordinary moments,
Divine repair appeared.
Barefoot and quiet,
rearranging her soul until everything felt lighter.

There was no special announcement.
No cheering.
Just a stillness in her mind.
A softness in her presence.
A deep knowing:
the worst had passed,
and yet—she had remained.
Not just surviving,
but awakening.

The miracle wasn't that the pain disappeared.
It was that she could now see herself—clearly—beyond it.

She had spent years trying to forget,
as if erasing the memories could undo the scars.
But redemption didn't ask her to forget.
It invited her to remember—
gently, truthfully, without shame.

It handed her the mirror,
asked her to look at the girl who survived

and say,
"You did not deserve what broke you.
But look at how you lived."

No longer searching for the mysterious,
Kyra began to recognize restoration in everyday moments—
in the sound of her laughter, unfiltered,
in tears shed without apology,
in silence no longer held in fear.

It was in the boundaries she no longer explained,
the peace she guarded like treasure,
the softness she finally gave herself permission to feel.

Wholeness, she realized, was not a destination.
It was a homecoming.
A return to herself.
To wholeness.
To the God who had waited patiently
while she hid behind survival.

It arrived not with fanfare, but with quiet resolve.
She saw it in the way she entered a room, head held high.
In the steadiness of her voice as she told the truth.
In the way she believed—
not just with her mind, but with her whole being—
that she was enough.

She no longer chased restoration.
It had been chasing her all along.
Woven into every tear,
tucked inside each rise from the ashes.

It had been there
the day she said no and meant it.
The day she stopped contorting for comfort.

The day she smiled—not to cover pain,
but because joy had finally made a home in her.

And with time, Kyra saw the truth:
renewal didn't erase her scars.
It redefined them—
turned them into witnesses.
Every mark, a monument to her becoming.

She hadn't noticed the transformation.
Because rebirth often grows quietly
in the cracks of surrender,
rooted in persistence,
blossoming in grace.

Wholeness looked like standing in front of the mirror
and seeing herself—not through the lens of pain,
or the harsh words of Rose—
but through the eyes of love.

She no longer questioned her worth.
She knew.
She was whole.
She was seen.
She was held.

The approval she once chased
was never in their hands.
It had always been etched
into the blueprint of her being
by the One who made her.

Renewal looked like emotional release—
not the absence of memory,
but the absence of bondage.
She was no longer gripped by rejection,

no longer paralyzed by fear.

Criticism came, but it didn't stick.
Old words—"too much," "not enough"—
lost their sting.
She believed her own voice now.
Steady. Rooted. Healed.

Peace had become her rhythm.
She no longer performed to be chosen.
She rested in being loved.
She no longer chased identity—
she embodied it.

She surrendered the pressure
to become someone else's version of worthy.
She laid it down—
at the feet of the One who had always called her His.

Recovery looked like breaking the cycles—
not just talking about it,
but living it.
She forgave and meant it.
Let go and felt it.
Freed herself, then offered freedom.

She was no longer just surviving.
She was guiding.
Her scars became signposts.
Her story became strategy.
She wasn't just free—
she helped others get free.

Redemption looked like purpose—bold and holy.
No more shrinking.
No more asking for permission to speak.

She walked in the authority of one who knows
she belongs.
She moved like a woman with fire in her bones.
She testified with power.
The shame had become a song.
The wounds, now weapons of truth.

Mending the pieces together looked like kindness toward herself.
She smiled more.
Rested without guilt.
Received joy without suspicion.

And healing looked like waking up
without the weight of yesterday's wounds
pulling her back.
Rose's voice had gone silent.
The shrinking had stopped.

She wasn't hiding anymore.
She was home.
In her body.
In her calling.
In her soul.

For the first time,
Kyra wasn't just existing—
she was alive.

And in that sacred stillness,
she felt it—

the arrival of peace.
Not thunderous.
Not grand.
But quiet.
Certain.

It didn't erase her past.
It redeemed it.
It didn't make life perfect.
It made her whole.

Healing didn't knock on the door.
It moved in.

And in the space where shame used to live,
there was now room—
for joy,
for peace,
for freedom.

She hadn't just healed.
She had become.
She was *whole*.

Reflection:

Healing doesn't always feel like a grand arrival.
Sometimes it's the moment you realize: I'm not bleeding where I used to.

Ask yourself:

- What evidence of healing is already showing up in your life?
- Are you still expecting healing to look like something loud or instant?
- How have you changed, even if no one else sees it yet?

Sometimes the proof of healing is in:

- The quiet.
- The breath you didn't hold.
- The memory that no longer breaks you.
- The peace you didn't think was possible.

Please use the space below to record your thoughts:

_____

_____

_____

_____

_____

_____

_____

_____

_____

_____

_____

_____

* * *

"Healing didn't knock—it entered quietly, day by day, breath by breath. I am not who I was. I am whole in places I once thought would never mend."

Chapter 10

I Am Redeemed by Faith, Not by Perfection

For years, Kyra saw her pain as something to erase.
A stain to be scrubbed away with enough time,
enough distance,
enough silence.
She believed wholeness meant forgetting—
that true freedom would come
only when the memories no longer haunted her,
when rejection no longer clung to her like a second skin.

But faith—
real, unshakable faith—
caused everything to move.

Faith opened her eyes to a truth she had never considered:
God never asked her to erase her past.
He intended to redeem it.

The wounds, the heartbreak, the hollow silences—
none of it had been wasted.
Every scar carried a story.

Every rejection shaped her resilience.
Every valley carved out the depth of her calling.

Through faith, Kyra no longer saw her pain as a mistake,
or a cruel twist of fate.
She saw it as preparation.
The fire that once threatened to consume her
had instead refined her.

Healing, she realized,
wasn't about pretending the pain never happened.
It wasn't about hiding the bruises
or numbing the ache.

Healing meant surrender.
It meant placing every shattered piece of her heart into God's hands
and trusting Him to do what only He could do—
transform it.
He makes beauty from ashes.
And in her life, He was doing just that.

And suddenly, Romans 8:28 wasn't just a verse to recite—
it was the foundation beneath her feet:

*"And we know that in all things God works for the good of those who love Him,
who have been called according to His purpose."* — *Romans 8:28*

God was working everything for her good—
the betrayal, the abandonment, the silence, the struggle.
The very pain she once begged God to remove
had become the tool He used to equip her,
strengthen her,
and position her to set others free.

She no longer viewed her scars with shame.
She saw them as evidence—

proof of God's faithfulness.
Proof that even in her darkest places,
He had never left.
He had been writing redemption into her story all along.

Then came the moment that solidified everything.

Kyra stood before a packed room—
women of all ages, all backgrounds,
each one carrying invisible burdens.

She held the microphone, scanning their faces,
and before she spoke a word,
she felt the weight of their longing.
The atmosphere pulsed with expectation.

And as her words filled the room,
she watched walls crumble.
Tears welled in the eyes of women
who, for the first time,
saw their own pain reflected in someone else's voice.

Chains broke.

Shoulders shook.

Deliverance swept in
like a wind through dry bones.

And in that holy moment,
Kyra no longer wished away her past.
She no longer questioned why she had endured what she did.
Because now, she knew.

If she hadn't walked through it,
she wouldn't be standing here—

breaking generational curses,
setting captives free,
telling the truth that heals.

For the first time,
she didn't just believe God had a purpose for her pain.
She knew it.

Her past wasn't a curse.
It was the platform for her calling.

And with a quiet exhale,
Kyra stood grounded.
Not in pride—
but in peace.

The kind of peace that comes
when you finally see your story through God's eyes.

The kind of peace that whispers,
"You made it out on purpose… for purpose."

She was no longer a woman hiding her scars.
She was a woman testifying through them.

Redeemed by faith—
not by perfection.

She didn't just feel restored.
She felt chosen.

"The little girl within didn't need to be erased, she needed to be embraced."

- Kimberely R. Allen

Reflection:

Faith doesn't just patch what was broken.
It rewrites the story, reintroduces you to yourself, and declares: You are not what happened to you.

Ask yourself:

- Have you accepted redemption, or are you still trying to earn restoration?
- What would it look like to stop rehearsing your shame and start walking in your salvation?
- Where has God already redeemed you—are you willing to see it?

Redemption means God looked at your mess and still said, "Mine."

Please use the space below to record your thoughts:

_____

_____

_____

_____

_____

_____

_____

_____

_____

_____

_____

_____

_____

_____

_____

_____

_____
_____
_____
_____
_____
_____
_____
_____
_____
_____
_____
_____
_____
_____
_____
_____
_____
_____
_____
_____
_____
_____
_____
_____
_____
_____
_____

* * *

*"My past does not cancel my promise. Faith is rewriting my story—one bold,
beautiful word at a time. What was lost is not gone; it's being redeemed.*

Chapter 11

I Silenced the Voice That Tried to Define Me

For years,
Rose had been more than just a voice in Kyra's mind—
she had been a force.
A relentless, insidious whisperer,
threading doubt through every inch of her soul,
wrapping chains around her heart with words
that felt more like truth than lies.

"You're not enough."
"You'll always be broken."
"God can't use someone like you."
"You are unlovable."

Kyra had grown so accustomed to Rose's voice
that she didn't know who she was without it.
Rose had become her inner critic.
Her shadow.
A voice born from childhood rejection
and the wounds inflicted by those who were supposed to love her.

The most dangerous thing about Rose?
Kyra believed her.

Rose didn't need to shout.
She whispered.
In the stillness of the night.
In the silence of loneliness.
She was there when Kyra second-guessed herself,
when she walked away from opportunities,
when she walked away at hello, afraid of goodbye.

Rose convinced her that peace was impossible.
That love would always be out of reach.
That she was destined to repeat the same pain that raised her.

Rose was the reason Kyra stayed silent when she should've
spoken.
The reason she settled for less—
convinced she couldn't ask for more.
The reason she turned away from moments
God had prepared just for her,
believing she wasn't worthy enough to walk in them.

And yet…
even in the darkness of self-doubt,
a quiet war was being waged.

God was working.

He counted every tear she cried in secret.
He saw her in the stillness, opening her Bible,
clinging to Psalms like oxygen.
He sat with her in therapy,
as she uncovered the roots of her pain.
He heard every desperate prayer,
whispered between sobs and exhaustion.

And He honored every trembling moment
when she dared to believe—just barely—that maybe…
she was more than the lies she'd been told.

God was planting something new.

And then came the moment—
a defining second that changed everything.

Kyra stood in front of the mirror,
staring at the woman reflected back.
For years, she had avoided her own gaze,
afraid of what she'd see.
Afraid she'd find proof that Rose was right.
That she was broken. Unworthy. Less than.

But tonight… something happened.
Something so special emerged from within.

She opened her mouth.
And for the first time in her life,
she spoke directly to the voice
that had tormented her for years.

"I know what you're trying to do, Rose."

Her hands gripped the edge of the bathroom sink.
Her body trembled—not with fear, but with resolve.
With truth.

"But you don't control me anymore."

The words didn't just leave her lips.
They thundered out of her soul.
It wasn't just a declaration.
It was an eviction notice.

A shift took place.
Something broke.

The torment.
The doubt.
The shame.
Everything Rose had ever whispered
began to lose its grip.

And Kyra felt it.
The weight lifted.
The power that voice once held over her mind,
her choices,
her identity—
began to crumble.

She saw Rose for what she truly was:
A distant thought of the past.
A distorted voice built on lies.
A defeated shadow that had masqueraded as truth for too long.

And in that beautiful moment,
Kyra made a decision:

She would no longer be bound.
She would no longer allow a wounded voice from her past
to dictate the path of her future.
She was a child of God—
chosen, loved, and set apart.

Kyra turned from the mirror,
not in avoidance,
but in triumph.

She had seen the enemy.
And she had declared victory.

In the days that followed,
she didn't just speak freedom.
She walked in it.

She filled her mind with God's Word.
And the more truth she absorbed,
the quieter Rose became.

Every time the whisper of doubt tried to return,
she answered it with Scripture:

> *"I am fearfully and wonderfully made."*
> *—Psalm 139:14*

> *"God has not given me a spirit of fear,*
> *but of power, love, and a sound mind."*
> *—2 Timothy 1:7*

> *"I am more than a conqueror through*
> *Christ who loves me."*
> *—Romans 8:37*

Day by day,
Kyra took back the territory
that once belonged to shame.

And then, one morning,
she realized something.

She woke up…
and Rose was silent.

For the first time,
the loudest voice in her mind
wasn't fear.
It wasn't doubt.

It was peace.

And with a deep, steady breath,
Kyra was liberated.

"She waited at the window for someone to return... never knowing she would one day become the woman who walked herself home."

- Kimberely R. Allen

Reflection:

You are not who the pain says you are.
You are not who abandonment says you are.
You are not even who you used to be.

You are who God calls you—even before you believe it yourself.

Ask yourself:

- What internal voices have tried to define your worth or identity?
- Whose voice still speaks louder than God's?
- What truths do you need to start speaking over yourself every day?

Silencing the old voice doesn't require shouting back. It requires agreement with the truth.

Please use the space below to record your thoughts:

_____
_____
_____
_____
_____
_____
_____
_____
_____
_____
_____
_____
_____
_____

_____
_____
_____
_____
_____
_____
_____
_____
_____
_____
_____
_____
_____
_____
_____
_____
_____
_____
_____
_____
_____
_____
_____
_____
_____
_____
_____
_____
_____
_____

* * *

"I have outgrown the words that once defined me. That voice no longer fits the woman I've become. I speak now with truth, with power, with freedom."

Chapter 12

I Fought the Battle And Purpose Has Emerged

Kyra didn't just survive the war—
she emerged with fire in her bones.

She wasn't the same woman
who once questioned her worth in the dark.
She had fought the voice that haunted her.
And she won.

But victory wasn't the end of the story.
It was the beginning of something greater.

She had scars, yes.
But they no longer whispered shame—
they spoke with authority.

Every lie she once believed had become fuel.
Fuel for the mission.
Fuel for the women still waiting to be free.

This was what the battle was for.

Not just her healing—
but her calling.

She didn't need a stage.
She didn't need applause.
She carried her deliverance like a banner—
quiet, bold, and holy.

Kyra had stepped into purpose,
and her life became a living trace of grace:
proof that broken places still bleed power
when God is in the story.

This wasn't just about silencing Rose anymore.
This was about living.
This was about breaking chains.

Kyra stood in front of a room full of women—
some with mascara-streaked cheeks,
others with arms crossed in defense,
all of them carrying private battles:
shame, fear, doubt, regret.

She saw it in their eyes—
the same weight she once carried.
The same war she used to lose.

But now... she was on the other side.

She wasn't just free.
She was dangerous.

She took a breath,
closed her eyes,
and whispered:
"Thank You, Lord."

This wasn't theory.
This was blood-bought, hell-fought testimony.

She hadn't just survived.
She had overcome.

She had crawled through depression.
Screamed in silence.
Wept until her pillow soaked through.
Doubted God.
Doubted herself.
Almost gave up more times than she could count.

But she was still standing.

Not because she was strong—
but because God is faithful.

She opened her mouth.
"I know what it's like to be held hostage
by a voice that isn't yours."

Her voice didn't shake—
it struck.

"I know what it's like to believe that voice
more than the voice of God.
But hear me—the enemy only has power
when we hand him the mic."

The room stirred.
And nothing was the same.

"Some of you have been dancing with your chains so long,
you don't even realize they're chains anymore.
You've made peace with the lies.

You've let shame dress up like identity.
But tonight…"
She stepped forward—
"…tonight, the voice loses its grip."

She didn't raise her voice.
She didn't need to.
The truth did the heavy lifting.

"Rose was never you.
That fear was never your future.
That pain was never your purpose."

She lifted her hands—
not in performance,
but in surrender.

"Tonight, I silence every lie that told you you're not enough.
Every whisper that said, 'You'll never break free.'
Every 'no' that came when God was shouting yes.
Every time fear tried to drown your faith.
Every moment rejection screamed louder than grace."

She paused.

"I know—because I was her.
I let Rose talk me out of purpose.
I let her convince me I was too broken, too dirty, too far gone."

A hush fell over the room.

"But then God.

God showed me—
deliverance isn't just a moment at the altar.
It's a war in your mind.

A daily fight.
A decision.
And I chose Him."

"And now… I walk in power."

The room went still.
But it wasn't silence.
It was reverence.

The kind of stillness that comes
when chains fall.
When lies lose their grip.
When women remember who they are.

Tears didn't just fall.
They flowed.

Some wept openly.
Others clenched their fists,
not in anger—
but because something deep inside was breaking.

Deliverance was happening.
Not at the altar—
but in the mind.

Kyra didn't call them to repeat a prayer.
She called them to make a choice.

"You don't have to walk out of here
the same way you came in.
You don't have to keep wearing
what was never yours to carry.
You don't have to keep answering
to a name God never gave you."

She stepped back—
not because she was done,
but because the Holy Spirit had taken over.

Kyra knew this was bigger than her voice.
This was the voice of truth.
Of freedom.
Of purpose awakened.

And as she watched women lift their heads,
eyes swollen but burning with new light,
she whispered again—

"This is what the battle was for."

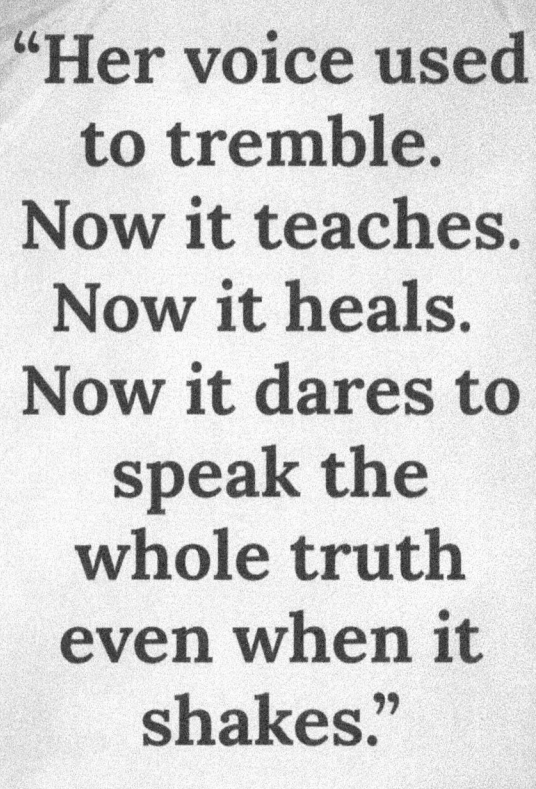

"Her voice used
to tremble.
Now it teaches.
Now it heals.
Now it dares to
speak the
whole truth
even when it
shakes."

- Kimberely R. Allen

Reflection:

Victory isn't just about what you overcome.
It's about what you carry out of the battle.

Ask yourself:

- What parts of your story once felt like defeat—but now carry purpose?
- How has your pain prepared you to help someone else?
- What did the storm awaken in you?

The win isn't always loud.
Sometimes it looks like finally understanding that your 'why' was woven through every wound.

Please use the space below to record your thoughts:

_____
_____
_____
_____
_____
_____
_____
_____
_____
_____
_____
_____
_____
_____
_____
_____

* * *

"My scars are not signs of defeat—they are proof I survived. The battle didn't break me; it built the strength I now walk in. I am purposely in motion."

Chapter 13

I Am Answering the Call to Freedom

She walked.

Not to clear her head—though sometimes that happened.
Not to get her steps in.
Not even for exercise.

She walked because that's where she met God.
The park was her sanctuary.
Her war room.
The wind, her counselor.
The quiet, her journal.

She didn't write her prayers—
she walked them out.
Step by step.
Word by word.

And on this particular day, the air felt different.

Not lighter.

Kimberely R. Allen

Not louder.
Just… free.

There was no heaviness pressing down on her.
No nagging thoughts circling like vultures.
No Rose.

Freedom, she realized, wasn't a grand declaration.
It was subtle, like morning light easing into a dark room.
It looked like ordering without second-guessing.
Like resting without earning it.
Like existing without apology.

It looked like her.

Not the polished version—
but the raw, radiant truth of who she had always been
beneath the rubble of rejection and roles.

She remembered the days she moved like a shadow.
When her worth was borrowed from others' opinions.
When "no" felt like betrayal,
and suppression was her shield.

A new perspective came to her mind.

She didn't just challenge the lies—
she stopped living according to them.

She spoke up when it felt awkward.
Chose softness when anger felt safer.
Let herself be celebrated without shrinking.
She stopped chasing closure from people who never held the key.

Every small act was rebellion against the old voice.

And with every step,
freedom wasn't just an idea—
it became her inheritance.

God had always been walking with her,
not pushing, not pulling—
just waiting.
For her to stop clinging to the familiar ache of survival.
For her to trust that healing didn't mean forgetting,
it meant forgiving.

Freedom didn't roar.
It unfolded.
In stillness. In steps. In sacred release.

And as the breeze circled around her like a knowing friend,
Kyra finally understood:

She wasn't trying to get somewhere anymore.

She was already here.

Reflection:

Freedom doesn't always come with fireworks.
Sometimes it starts with a whisper: "There is more."

Ask yourself:

- Have you mistaken comfort for freedom?
- What does freedom look like for you—emotionally, spiritually, relationally?
- Are you willing to walk into freedom, even if it costs you your old identity?

This is your moment to step out of what you've known
and step into what you were always made for.

Please use the space below to record your thoughts:

_____

_____

_____

_____

_____

_____

_____

_____

_____

_____

_____

_____

_____

_____

_____

_____

* * *

"I was never meant to stay in chains. I hear freedom calling me by name, and I'm answering boldly, without apology. I was made to soar."

Chapter 14

I Am Ready to Tell My Story

That night, something in Kyra's spirit wouldn't let her rest.

The house was quiet—
the kind of quiet that made space for the unsaid.
A holy hush, thick with memory,
thin with breath.

And in that stillness, she felt it—
an ache, soft but steady,
pressing gently against her chest.
Not loud. Not frantic.
Just… insistent.

She didn't reach for her journal with a plan.
It was instinct, not intention.
A movement born from somewhere deeper than thought.

Her fingers brushed the page.
She hesitated.
Not because she didn't know what to write—

but because the words had been waiting,
and she knew once they came,
they wouldn't stop.

She let her hand move.
No outline.
No filter.
Just truth.

Each line was a release—
a confession wrapped in rhythm,
a memory breaking open like dawn.

This wasn't a letter.
It wasn't a chapter.
It was a reckoning.

She wrote for the men who had never had a safe place to fall
apart—
the fighters who were never taught how to feel.
The carriers. The quiet ones.
The strong who learned how to disappear inside their own
resilience.

She wrote for the fathers who held grief behind their backs,
for the sons whose softness was mistaken for weakness,
for the husbands who bore the weight of the world in silence.
She wrote for the man who needed a mirror but was only ever
handed armor.
For the brother who shows up, holds it down, and breaks in private.

This was for them, too.
Not to expose them—
but to remind the men that they, too, deserve to be seen.

Kyra thought of the boy who had never been allowed to cry.

The Little Girl Within

The woman who had never been asked, "Are you okay?"
The friend who laughed too loudly to hide the ache.

Her pen moved like prayer.
A slow, sacred offering.

She wrote for the ones who had always been told
to "man up" before they were ever taught how to heal.
She wrote for the girl who believed
her silence was safer than her voice.
She wrote for the version of herself
who didn't yet know it was okay to break.

The lines spilled out like breath:

You are not weak for being wounded.
You are not invisible just because you've been silent.
You're allowed to heal.
You're allowed to cry.
You're allowed to come undone
in front of a God who holds you together.

She paused,
the ink trembling where her hand met the page.

The truth was settling in her bones.
This wasn't just for someone else.
It was for her, too.

She hadn't expected this.
Hadn't prepared for the release that came with it.
But the moment the pen stopped moving,
something else began.

She thought she would feel lighter.
But instead—she felt a shift.

Kimberely R. Allen

Not relief. Revelation.

The writing had opened a door she didn't know was locked.
A deeper layer rising from within,
unfolding quietly like an invitation.

This letter... this chapter...
wasn't the end of something.

It was the beginning of a new kind of recovery—
one she hadn't planned,
but one she could no longer deny.

Because in naming their scars,
she had uncovered more of her own.
And in writing the truth,
she had given herself permission
to feel it.
To face it.
To finally be free from the weight
she didn't even realize she was still carrying.

Kyra closed the journal,
but the story wasn't finished.

The house was still quiet,
but inside her, something had shifted.
A deeper truth had been stirred,
one that couldn't be unwritten.

She sat there a moment longer,
hands resting over the pages
that had just poured from her soul.
It wasn't just a release.
It was a return.

To herself.
To her voice.
To the call she could no longer ignore.

And in that sacred stillness, she knew—
she wasn't finished.

Not with the mending.
Not with the writing.
Not with the purpose that was slowly, surely
rising to the surface.

Reflection:

God chose you.
Someone else needs your breakthrough.

Ask yourself:

- What part of your life have you been afraid to speak or write about?
- Could your obedience unlock healing in someone else?
- Are you willing to be seen—even if it wasn't part of your plan?

The words may cost you something.
But they will give others permission they need.

Please use the space below to record your thoughts:

_____
_____
_____
_____
_____
_____
_____
_____
_____
_____
_____
_____
_____
_____
_____
_____
_____

---

* * *

"The story I never planned to tell became the truth someone else needed. My voice is no longer hidden. I speak because I've survived."

Chapter 15

I Am Releasing What Was Never Mine to Carry

She thought she had already let it go.

She had written the words.
Spoken the truth.
Testified in rooms that mocked her.
Prayed over wounds she thought had scabbed.

But recovery doesn't always flow in a straight line.
And release doesn't come in one wave.

Sometimes, it comes quiet.
Waiting for the stillness.
Waiting for the moment when survival no longer holds the mic.
When you're no longer fighting to breathe—just breathing.

She had inked her story into pages,
but some things were still carved into bone.

The betrayal she never gave voice to.
The guilt she never knew she was allowed to put down.

The people she forgave—but never truly released.

Her hands had opened.
But her heart… still clenched.

And this was the moment God reached for that last locked door—
the one she guarded like it held her together,
the one that said, don't go there… not yet.

But He did.

And in that moment—
knees tucked to her ribs,
tears falling in silence—
she wasn't just healing.

She was being freed.

Her deliverance didn't roar.
No choir. No organ. No audience.
Just breath.
Just the sound of a soul finally exhaling in God's presence.

She didn't ask Him to take it.
She simply confessed she was tired of carrying it.

The weight of expectation.
The role of the strong one.
The script of always being "okay."
The pressure to perform instead of living truth.

She said things she had never dared to say aloud.
Not because God couldn't handle them—
but because she had never given herself permission to.

And still—He stayed.

The Little Girl Within

He didn't rush her.
Didn't fix her.
Didn't silence her trembling.

He just listened.

And when the words ran out—
she wasn't met with shame.
She was met with safety.

"You can put it down now," the Holy Spirit said.
"You were never meant to carry this into the next season."

So she did.
Not in a flood, but in a slow, sacred unraveling.

She laid down the guilt she had worn like armor.
The shame she carried like a shell.
The grief she tucked beneath her laughter.
The memory of who never came back.

She uttered names—
some to forgive, some to finally release.

She mourned the moments she'd never get back.
Released the apologies she never received.
Grieved the girl inside her who kept showing up when no one
else did.

And she wept.

Not the sobs of collapse—
but the tears of surrender.
The tears of a woman safe enough to fall apart.
And brave enough to rise differently.

This wasn't breakdown.
This was worship.
Holy. Honest.
A release no longer delayed.

She didn't feel haunted anymore by what she survived.
She felt honored to still be here.
Still breathing.
Still becoming.

She had lived for so long in the shadows of others' expectations,
their projections draped over her like borrowed clothes.

But now…
she knew better.

Transformation was never about proving her worth.
It was about standing,
whole and holy,
in the truth of who she had become—
even if no one else noticed.

God did.
And that was enough.

Kyra didn't fall apart because she was fragile.
She let go because she was finally safe enough to do so.
Because she had learned that letting go isn't weakness—
it's worship.

This is the divine part of restoration.
The hidden part.
The part where you stop pretending something doesn't hurt—
just because you survived it.

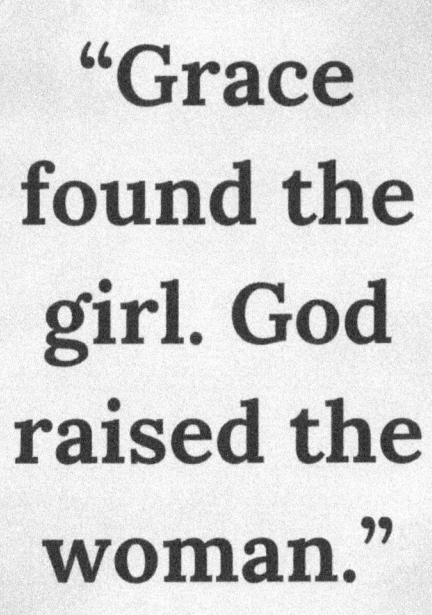

"Grace found the girl. God raised the woman."

- Kimberely R. Allen

Reflection:

Release is not weakness—it's courage in motion.
Letting go doesn't mean you've failed.
It means you've finally made room for peace.

Ask yourself:

- What are you still gripping that's no longer serving your growth?
- Is it strength, or is it fear disguised as endurance?
- What would happen if you trusted God with all of it?

You're not losing control—you're gaining clarity.
Release is the doorway to restoration.

Please use the space below to record your thoughts:

_____

_____

_____

_____

_____

_____

_____

_____

_____

_____

_____

_____

_____

_____

_____

_____

_____

* * *

"I release what I cannot carry into the hands of the One who can. This letting go is not a loss—it's my liberation."

Chapter 16

I Am Not Lost Despite My Breaking

She had survived so much.

The trauma.
The silence.
The lies.
Even Rose.

But this?
This was different.

This wasn't a breakdown of memory or fear.
This was a slow unraveling from the inside out.

Because nothing was technically wrong.
No sudden loss.
No diagnosis.
No betrayal.

Just a quiet ache that refused to leave.
A hollowing out in her soul that left her wondering—

What am I even doing?

She spoke it out loud one afternoon, parked outside her church.
The same church where she preached, taught, served—
where her title still rang louder than her peace.

Her computer bag rested on the passenger seat.
Her to-do list blinked from her phone.

She had a board meeting to attend.
A sermon to prepare.
A women's event to lead.

And still—she felt… empty.

Not because she was ungrateful.
But because she was tired.
Tired of trying on every version of purpose
only to find none of them quite fit.

She had tried it all.
Fashion.
Writing.
Ministry.
Degrees.

Each path brought fruit—
but also questions.

And lately, the only one that stuck was:
"God, if I'm this gifted, why am I still this confused?"

She sat still, hands locked around the steering wheel.
Tears rose, but they didn't fall.

Not yet.

The Little Girl Within

This wasn't a collapse.
It was exhaustion.
A weariness born from the weight of obedience
mixed with the ache of uncertainty.

She was worn.

Worn from trying to follow God
while constantly wondering if she was even hearing Him right.

Worn from every prophetic word that never came to pass.
Worn from every well-meaning voice declaring her calling—
but never teaching her how to survive the waiting.

She had been obedient.
She had been bold.
She had been still.

But there was something deeper—
a truth she hadn't yet named aloud:

Maybe I missed it.
Not because I disobeyed…
but because I was afraid.

Afraid to disappoint people.
Afraid to disappoint God.
Afraid to start again—again.
Afraid to leave what was safe
for what might actually be hers.

And now, with years behind her,
and more questions than answers,
she was wondering—

Did I wait too long?

Did purpose pass me by
while I was trying to be everything for everyone else?

She wasn't looking for lightning.
Or a burning bush.
She just needed to know He was still listening.

And in the stillness,
He spoke.

Not with plans.
Not with fireworks.
Not with blueprints.

But with presence.

No thunder.
No booming voice.
Just the faintest expression behind the ache—

"You didn't miss it."

"I've been weaving purpose through every piece—
even the pauses.
Even the fear.
Even the years you thought were wasted."

Her shoulders dropped.
Her breath slowed.
One long exhale she hadn't realized
she'd been holding for half her life.

Maybe purpose wasn't waiting at the end of some grand staircase.
Maybe it had always been walking beside her.

Maybe it wasn't about doing more—

but recognizing what had already been done.

She didn't feel powerful yet.
She didn't feel like dancing.
But she did feel… held.

And that was enough for now.

Because sometimes,
the holiest thing a woman can say is—

"God, I'm tired."

Kyra hadn't fallen into rebellion.
She had simply reached her limit.
She hadn't run away from God.
She had just sat down for a moment,
unsure how to keep going.

And He didn't scold her for it.
He didn't ask her to try harder.

He met her there.
And when He did,
He didn't just welcome her back.

He released a second wind into her bones.

Her breaking point wasn't failure.
It was a holy pause.

And from that place—
He began restoring what she thought had unraveled for good.

Reflection:

You didn't break because you were weak.
You broke because something heavy had to be released.

And still—you're here.

Ask yourself:

- What was your breaking point, and what did it teach you?
- How did God meet you in your most fragile place?
- What did your breaking point build in you?

Breaking is not the end—it's the beginning of becoming.

Please use the space below to record your thoughts:

_____
_____
_____
_____
_____
_____
_____
_____
_____
_____
_____
_____
_____
_____
_____
_____

_____
_____
_____
_____
_____
_____
_____
_____
_____
_____
_____
_____
_____
_____
_____
_____
_____
_____
_____
_____
_____
_____
_____
_____
_____
_____
_____
_____
_____
_____
_____
_____

* * *

"I met the edge, and didn't fall, I found faith. What tried to break me only revealed what still lives in me: resilience, purpose, and a reason to rise again."

Chapter 17

I Am Still Standing

Kyra had come a long way.

She had held the hand of the little girl who once hid in silence.
She had peeled back the layers of shame and called herself worthy.
She had stood before the mirror—no longer shrinking—
finally believing what God said about her.

But restoration doesn't always mean the battle is over.
Sometimes, it simply means you've entered a new one.

It doesn't always return as pain.
Sometimes it comes in the silence between victories.
In the spaces where joy lives… and questions sneak in quietly.

That's when the changes began.

At first, it was small.

The absence of Rose's voice felt like peace.
But it wasn't peace.

It was preparation.

Because Rose hadn't disappeared.
She had evolved.

And Kyra didn't see it—
Not right away.

There were glimpses.
Moments that felt familiar but slightly off.
A doubt that didn't sound afraid…
It sounded confident.

It didn't beg.
It baited.

And that was the first sign.

The little girl…
who used to cower in the corners of her mind was gone.
But in her place stood someone else—
Not a child.
A teenager.

She arrived in the most ordinary moment.

Kyra had just finished ministering.
The altar had been full.
Tears had flowed.
Testimonies had been shared.

She should have felt light.
Free.
Covered in glory.

But instead, she sat in her car alone,

keys in her lap, heart pounding against nothing.

That's when she heard it.

The voice.
Still Rose—but different.

Sharper.
Smarter.
Wrapped in confidence, laced with sarcasm.

"You handled the childhood stuff well," she said.
"But what about your teenage and adulthood years?
The friendships that failed.
The boys who used you.
The rejection that felt like love.
The choices that still rummage in your mind?"

It caught her off guard.

Like finding an old photo you didn't remember taking—
but somehow couldn't forget.

This wasn't the voice of fear.
This was the voice of accusation.
And it didn't whisper.

It mocked.

"They cheer for you now…" Rose continued,
"but you know better.

Remember when you asked your husband
why he loved you?
Why he stayed?
How he could still hold you

when you felt…
so uneducated,
so unworthy,
so incapable…
of helping your own children with their homework?"

The silence after her words hit harder than the voice itself.

Then, a final blow—quiet, but cruel:
"You never really believed you were enough.
Not then.
Not now."

Kyra blinked.
Tried to shake it off.
Tried to pray.
Tried to call it fatigue.

But deep in her spirit, a truth stirred—
This isn't just a memory.
This isn't just flesh, family, or fatigue.
This is war.

This is the battlefield of faith.

The words didn't sting.
They stuck.

Before she could rebuke them,
before she could journal or worship or quote a Scripture—
something inside her agreed.

Not all the way.
Just enough to make her question.

She didn't drive home.

The Little Girl Within

She drove past it.
Past the church.
Past the noise.
And into the parking lot of a park,
where her worship playlist paused mid-song.

She turned it off.
Turned her phone to silent.
Ignored the calls from her husband.
Let the text messages sit unread.

And stared at the ceiling of her car like it owed her an answer.

Maybe they don't see me.
Maybe I'm still the extra one.
Still disposable.

And just like that—
faith trembled.

She didn't curse God.
She didn't throw away her calling.

She just didn't answer it that day.

She sat in the silence.
Not bitter.
Just tired.

She gripped the steering wheel like it was the only thing keeping her
from disappearing.

And said words she never thought she'd say again:
"Maybe she was right."

And somewhere inside—

where healing once lived—
a door creaked open.

And an older Rose walked through it.
Not screaming.
Not gloating.

Just… watching.
Waiting.

But Kyra didn't flinch.
Not this time.
She no longer bowed to the past of who she used to be.
She simply kept walking.
Past the shame.
Past the fear.
Past the version of herself that had once called silence safety.

Because freedom, she would soon learn, was only the beginning.

There would come a new kind of stretching—
one that didn't look like survival,
but surrender.
One that asked her to *merge* her becoming
with someone else's.

To lead and to be led.
To be strong and still soft.
To make room for love
without shrinking who she was.

Because healing had made her whole—
but partnership would ask:
Can you stay whole when you are no longer alone?

She wasn't searching for rescue anymore.

But she was searching for a new beat—
How to walk alongside someone
without losing the sound of her own steps.

The battle within had quieted.
But the *new* questions about belonging,
about ministry, marriage, and identity—
they were only beginning to rise.

And so, Kyra stepped forward again.
Not into war.
But into a new world.
One where love and calling collided.
One where her becoming continued.

A new chapter was stirring—
not one she expected,
but one she could no longer ignore.
Because sometimes, the real becoming
begins after the breakthrough.

And somewhere between calling and connection,
Kyra's journey continued…
as she faced a new question:

How do you stay whole when everything around you is merging together?

Reflection:

Faith isn't always pretty.
Sometimes it limps. Sometimes it cries.
But it keeps showing up.

Ask yourself:

- When has your faith been most tested?
- How did you keep going when belief felt impossible?
- What does faith look like for you now, after the fire?

This battlefield didn't break you.
It built your trust in ways comfort never could.

Please use the space below to record your thoughts:

_____

_____

_____

_____

_____

_____

_____

_____

_____

_____

_____

_____

_____

_____

_____

_____

_____

_____

* * *

"My fight is not flesh—it's faith. Even when I'm weary, I stand in the fire with hope as my weapon. I may bend, but I will not break."

A Letter to the Called

Dear Called,

This letter marks the shift—the turning point. It's the moment I decided to stop looking back and stop giving the past permission to steal from my future.

I almost lost you. I almost let the weight of expectations, disappointments, and unhealed wounds bury you beneath a version of yourself that was never meant to exist. For too long, I carried shame that didn't belong to me. I wore masks to make others comfortable and convinced myself that shrinking was the safest way to survive. But survival is not the same as freedom.

And now, I choose freedom.

I choose to see myself the way God sees me: whole, worthy, and loved. I choose to speak life over myself—not because I need anyone's permission, but because I've finally learned to listen to the voice of truth. This freedom, this release from fear, is mine to claim.

It wasn't handed to me by others, and it can't be taken away. I am free because I choose to be.

I'm free to live boldly. Free to love without restraint. Free to walk confidently in the calling God placed on my life.

I've let go—not just with words, but in action—of everything and everyone that kept me bound. I will no longer apologize for my growth. I will no longer question whether I deserve joy. I will no longer wait for approval to walk in my purpose.

To the woman reading this who has spent years waiting for someone else to set her free—hear me clearly: your freedom is not in their hands. It never was. Stop waiting for closure that may never come. Stop handing your identity to people who were never meant to define you. You are already enough. Start walking like it. Start living like it. Start believing it.

I am done asking for permission to be who I am. And so are you.

With love and boldness,
Kyra

Acknowledgments

To my God:

The Author of my story. The Keeper of my soul. The One who never walked away—even when I did. This book is Yours. Every word. Every tear. Every healed wound. You rescued her from the shadows. You taught me how to breathe again, to believe again, to become. Thank You for calling me worthy even when I felt invisible. Thank You for turning pain into purpose—and purpose into pages.

To my husband, Jonathan W. Allen, Sr.:

My angel. You are the love of my life, the calm in my chaos, the safe place my soul calls home. For 43 years, you've walked beside me—in love, in laughter, in faith, and in fire. In this season, where I had to write, reflect, and often pull away to face what was buried, you never made me feel guilty for needing space. Instead, you covered me in prayer and wrapped me in patience.

You are not only the man who loves me really well—you are the quiet strength behind every bold step I've taken. Your understanding has been my oil. Your devotion, my anchor. Thank you for loving me completely—not just as your wife, but as a woman healing, becoming, and remembering. You are my greatest gift. My answered prayer.

To my son, Jonathan W. Allen, Jr.:

Some moments are holy. That day in the British Virgin Islands was one of them.

We were both ministering, and after I spoke to the women during the afternoon session, God gave you a word—clear, prophetic, and undeniable. You wrote it down and handed it to me. On that paper, it simply read: God said, this is your next book: "The Little Girl Within."

I still remember how those words stared back at me, confirming what had been stirring deep inside. Your obedience to God's voice at that moment was more than a prophetic gesture—it was the divine spark that set this book in motion. Thank you for listening. Thank you for writing it down. Thank you for believing in me—and in what God was birthing through me. I love you.

To Minister Lakeisa Arrington:

There are people God sends not just to walk with you—but to war with you. You were one of those people for me. You became my anchor, my encourager, my trusted voice of truth. You stood with me through the stops and starts, the rewrites and the reawakening. You reminded me that this story was worth telling—even when I doubted my voice.

You didn't just help me organize chapters; you helped me organize my courage. You pushed me to press in when I wanted to pull back. You challenged me to write, then rewrite, then rewrite again—because you believed there was more in me. You were my rock in this writing season, and I will never forget the grace and grit you carried on my behalf. Thank you for being one of the reasons The Little Girl Within made it to the finish line.

To Prophetess Carla Clark:

Thank you for your obedience to the Spirit of God. At the Women of Worth Conference 2024, you bent down boldly and spoke the words that pierced through time and touched the root of my soul: "The little girl in you is gone." In that moment, something broke—and something beautiful began. That word was more than a declaration. It was a release. It was the confirmation that healing had come and that it was time to tell the story. Because you obeyed God, I was inspired to write this book. Because you spoke, I found the courage to speak, too. I will forever be grateful for your voice, your obedience, and your prophetic assignment in my life. You were part of the birthing process of this message, and I honor you for it.

To my Connect Church family:

Thank you for covering me in prayer and surrounding me with love through every season—especially this one. To the women of Connect: your words, your presence, your encouragement have carried me farther than you know. You gave me the freedom to be fully me—flawed, healing, transparent—and you thanked me for doing the very thing I once feared: telling the truth out loud. In your love, I found room to grow. In your prayers, I found the strength to keep writing. This book carries pieces of your encouragement on every page. I'm grateful beyond words.

About the Author

Pastor Kimberely R. Allen—affectionately known as "Lady Kim"—is a transformational leader, preacher, certified Christian counselor, and author dedicated to helping others heal, grow, and walk in purpose. With over 40 years in ministry and mentorship, she empowers women to rise beyond limitations and live boldly in obedience to God.

A proud GED graduate at 40 and valedictorian of Givens Bible College, Pastor Allen went on to earn a B.A. in Biblical Studies and Church Management and a Master of Divinity from Virginia Union University. She serves as an Associate Pastor at Connect Church in Waldorf, Maryland, where she co-leads with her husband, Dr. Jonathan W. Allen, Sr.

She is the founder of More Than A First Lady, a movement uplifting multidimensional women, and the author of Living in Two Worlds – Destined for Change, Destined for Change: The Guided Journal, and her newest release, The Little Girl Within.

Through her ministry, books, and businesses—including Finally Talls by KYRA and God's Hot Off the Press—Lady Kim continues to inspire, equip, and uplift the next generation of women walking toward healing and legacy.

www.ingramcontent.com/pod-product-compliance
Lightning Source LLC
Chambersburg PA
CBHW051148120626
46547CB00012B/991